W9-BSL-993

Few could guide us as well through dark moments toward wholeness. It takes a master storyteller and an extraordinarily sensitive soul to speak about loss and happiness in proximity to one another. Maria Sirois, by drawing on personal experience, research, and a lot of heart, can help us all navigate through life's most difficult experiences, so that we can find our way to safety, and even to happiness.

Tal Ben-Shahar, author of *Happier*

Maria Sirois is a born storyteller and "A Short Course in Happiness After Loss" is full of them, many from unlikely places, like the ground beneath her feet. Maria can extract a story from a rock in the road and such is her talent that we will happily bend down with her when she picks it up, turns it over, and tells us why this particular rock is so important. In the process, she tells us why we're important, too. This is a delicious book, full of truth and generosity and the kind of no-holds-barred honesty that characterizes Maria in person and on the page.

Phyllis Theroux, author of *The Journal Keeper*

What a wonderful book this is! Full of insight drawn from the author's clinical practice, *A Short Course in Happiness After Loss* deserves a place on your shelf next to *When Things Fall Apart*, *Broken Open*, and *The Year of Magical Thinking*. Beautifully written and tenderly observed, Maria Sirois' meditation on loss and resilience will help you through your darkest hours and fill your heart again with joy.

Mark Matousek, author of *When You're Falling, Dive*

This book tells us how to love truly, fully, and completely in the face of suffering and loss. Maria Sirois writes of her own losses and the losses of others she accompanies in her work as a therapist and teacher. This is a book of beauty and grace, a book that teaches us that happiness waits patiently for those who seek it.

Sherri Mandell, author of *The Blessing of a Broken Heart*

Stunned by the death of her 48-year-old brother, Maria Sirois asks how we summon our strengths to survive the agonies of this world. And she answers her question with stories of resilience from her own deeply felt experiences, amplified by poetry and the spiritual wisdom of the great sages. A trustworthy guide, she earns our confidence through courageous self-revelation. Rather than tuning out encounters with loss and suffering in her life and the lives of others, Maria has gathered them close, allowed them to transform her, and she has developed a set of profound lessons to teach what she has learned along the way. She reminds us, "We suffer. None of us is spared." In her short course, Maria gives us permission to confront suffering directly, while reminding us of our resilience, capacity to love, and our ability to endure.

Richard M. Berlin, author of *Practice* and *Secret Wounds*

How can we live with deep grief and still find meaning and happiness? It may seem impossible, but — drawing from her experiences and those of many people she has worked with — Maria shows us that this can happen. In her unique voice, poetic and heartfelt, she teaches us that there are no recipes for recovering from tragedy, but that we can choose how we want to be in the face of loss and learn to accept the puzzling but real coexistence of great pain and great joy in our life.

Margarita Tarragona, author of *Positive Identities: Narrative Practices and Positive Psychology*

Wise, real, and clear, this book offers a way into what we all have to do sooner or later — live alongside death. The words are not prescriptive, giving a pat recipe for managing loss and pain. Instead, with compassion rooted in experience, Maria unwraps little bubbles of hope with each story, honoring the raw truth of grief and the possibility of life waiting in the wings to resurface. If you're trying to figure out how to live in the face of death, and need a rudder to hold onto, grab this book.

Megan McDonough, author of *Radically Receptive Meditation*

Every grief is piercingly unique, and every one of us picks our own path through. What a lifeline to have Maria by our sides, presenting some universal human truths as signposts to guide us, tossing us the lifelines of wisdom and humor as we navigate to a new normal and rediscover light and grace.

Janet Reich Elsbach, blogger: *A Raisin and A Porpoise*

A SHORT COURSE IN HAPPINESS AFTER LOSS

(and Other Dark, Difficult Times)

Maria Sirois, Psy.D.

A SHORT COURSE IN HAPPINESS AFTER LOSS

(and Other Dark, Difficult Times)

Maria Sirois, Psy.D.

Green Fire Press

Housatonic, Massachusetts

Copyright © Maria Sirois, 2016.

Properly footnoted quotations of up to 500 sequential words may be used without permission, granted the total number of words quoted does not exceed 2,000. For longer quotations, or for a greater number of total words, please contact Green Fire Press: www.greenfirepress.com info@greenfirepress.org

Cover design by Adam Michael Rothberg
Cover image and Kintsugi pot by Dick Lehman
Page design by Anna Myers Sabatini

Green
Fire
Press

Library of Congress Control Number: 2016934171
ISBN 978-0-9861980-3-8

Green Fire Press
PO Box 377 Housatonic MA 01236

For R. and J.

Contents

Introduction 1

Part One: Loss..7

Choice...8

Lost...12

Breathe 15

Crazytown 20

True Hope...26

The Stories We Tell Ourselves...........................31

What We Feel 36

The Gift of Sight..40

Facing Fear 44

Why Me? 50

Whiplash...54

Loneliness 58

Where the Hell is That White Horse?................ 64

Exile 69

The Art of Losing 74

Part Two: Happiness...81

AND..82

Heaven Within Hell 87

Heaven Within Hell Part 2................................91

What Happiness Looks Like 95

Love..99

The Surround of Love: Loving Ourselves First....104

Grounded Optimism.......................................108

Courage..113

The Choir 118

Holding on and Letting Go...............................121

Becoming True.. 126

Undefended Hearts 130

This Meeting, One Chance...................... 136

The World Will Rise to Meet You.....................140

A New Story... 146

A Final Note 151

Notes to Self..152

Suggested Resources 156

Acknowledgments 158

Everything is Going to be All Right

By Derek Mahon

How should I not be glad to contemplate
the clouds clearing beyond the dormer window..?
There will be dying, there will be dying,
but there is no need to go into that...
The sun rises in spite of everything
and the far cities are beautiful and bright...
Everything is going to be all right.

Introduction

A few years ago my younger brother, John, a doctor, died after a ten-week struggle with pancreatic cancer. In October of 2010 he flew north from his home in North Carolina to celebrate my 50th birthday with me. Within four months I found myself standing in front of hundreds of his friends and colleagues offering a closing eulogy for his memorial service. As I walked to the podium, my hands twitching from iron-heavy sorrow, a thought crossed my mind: "How do we do this?" How do we find the courage to bury each other or survive the myriad agonies of this world — batterings, car collisions, plane crashes, chronic illness, job loss, betrayal, loss of a home, a body part, a friend — and find our way back into life, more specifically back into a life that resonates with hope, and love, and happiness? How do we rise, when darkness comes close?

This question is an old one in my world. I first found myself consciously asking it in my final year of training in graduate school while working as an intern at Dana-Farber Cancer Institute in Boston. There, with six other psychology interns, I met and treated scores of children facing cancer and other blood diseases and watched as some families fell apart and others became stronger. What did they know, those families who did well — who stayed mentally and emotionally intact, who remained present and were able to face reality while celebrating small moments of uplift — as their sons or daughters underwent treatments that in and of themselves might be fatal? And how did they find peace or a sense of happiness again once the battle with cancer had been lost? As a clinical psychologist, working in the field of death and dying, these questions were foundational to my work. What was it about those resilient families and how could I teach their wisdom to others?

In the last decade my work has shifted to a related focus. I now travel extensively, lecturing, teaching and consulting about the intersection of positive psychology — the study of what works and who we are at our best — and of resilience. My lectures focus on happiness, mindfulness, and the upward spiral of post-traumatic growth. My audiences have broadened to include professionals, business owners, work teams, volunteer groups, and adults of every age and stage. Still, at every event, almost everyone wants to know what those families at the Farber demonstrated: how to develop a deep capacity to grow even when life throws us its worst.

If I am honest with myself, though, these questions were in me long before that year of training at Dana-Farber. At nineteen I witnessed the struggle of my aunt to love life after the loss of her youngest son, Tommy, to brain cancer. Much before that, I felt the deep pull of sorrow surround our family when my father's father died of multiple myeloma. I was a toddler then, my parents still quite young themselves, and that loss fractured us for a time. I had a childhood bookended by cancer and figuring out how to thrive after a death became a focus of mine along the current of my youth. Attention to what we know as the field of resilience came to define the work I've chosen, the books I've absorbed and the friends I gather with; it is the gold I have sought in the mines of the living.

Walking up to the podium those years ago, holding my brother Johnny's eulogy in my hand, seeing in front of me his teenage children, my parents, his wife, our older brother, and the sea of faces of those who he had treated and those he had loved, I knew that moment would change many of us. And I found myself praying as I adjusted the microphone and stilled my hands that it would change me for the good...that if nothing else I would learn something more about living with suffering such that I might move back toward joy, and in so doing help others.

"There will be dying," poet Derek Mahon writes, and sometimes, he suggests, there is no need to go into that. There are days, months even, when life is in flow and it shimmers; we can move through our days with a lilting ease. In those times of respite and beneficence we do well to focus on the bounty around us and let lie for a time the great sorrows of the world. As we do so we refill the well within us.

And yet, to find the sun that rises in spite of everything — in other words, to find our way into delight and uplift even as the pains of the world surge — we must do our best to choose happiness. We must actively choose resilience. We must elect to craft a life that thrives. And it helps to know how to do that. That is what this book is for — those times, that quest.

The first half of the book offers considerations written from the perspective of loss or from those times when we are shuttered by darkness and strain. They illustrate the significant elements of that territory and address what happens to most of us in the hard moments: what crazy can look like, the myths we carry about "doing it right," and how awful awful can feel. The second half is written from the frame of happiness: how grounded optimism is gained, what an undefended heart looks like, and how heaven appears in the lives we are already living, sometimes with simply the tiniest of evidence.

This is not memoir, though I do reference my own battles from time to time. It presents a curriculum of sorts; a survey of what we would do well to understand as we head into times of high stress or the press of life becomes overwhelming.

Each reflection addresses a central theme that stands alone and yet a larger landscape will begin to appear as we read through: there is no life in which happiness and suffering exist separate from the other. The move toward greater happiness is an effort in which we carry evidence of our sufferings, just as each field of wheat or valley of bluebells grows directly upon the debris of what has been. There is no other land but the land that holds both; there is no other life but one in which our joys and our sufferings flow into and from each other.

May these words, gathered from personal moments of upheaval and from years of teaching the art and science of resilience, aid you in your journey.

May you discover that you aren't alone in feeling how difficult this all can be.

And may together we come to see that even with the great sorrow of this world everything, on some days, is possibly, astonishingly, all right.

— *Maria*

PART ONE
LOSS

*"Our greatest freedom is the freedom
to choose our attitude."*

~ Viktor Frankl

Choice

Trophy in hand, I skipped down Beechwood
Drive back to my home. June, 1972. I was 11
years old and it was the end of a great day. I had
won the "Outstanding 6th Grade Girl Award" at
Charlton Heights Elementary School, a school I
had transferred to 18 months prior. At that time in
my life trophies and recognition meant everything.
They helped me feel worthy, gave me a sense that I
mattered. It would be years before I would under-
stand the term "perfectionist," and much longer
before I knew to how to recover from trophy-hunt-
ing disease but that day I was nothing but happy.
The sun shone. My teachers liked me. I had gold in
my hands. Mom and dad would be proud. I walked
through the garage door, up the three steps into our
kitchen, waltzed into the living room to find my
brother, Johnny, crying, my older brother Joe, angry,
and my mom wracked, her shoulders hunched, tear

stains smudging the makeup on her face. I stopped abruptly, my trophy dangling down, and heard my mother speak. Our dog, Buffy, had been killed that afternoon. She had gotten out, chased a truck, and become caught under a tire. She was gone.

Stunned would describe my reaction in that moment. In the grand scheme of things this was perhaps not an earth-shattering loss. But it was a shock nonetheless and a sudden upheaval of what felt normal and easeful in our lives. Our first pet, Buffy, had been with us about a year, and that year of having a four-footed friend in our lives screeched to an end.

Staring in disbelief at my mother, the weight of the news pulling me to the floor, I understood three very powerful teachings in a heartbeat. 1) Good things don't protect us from bad things. 2) Bad things happen randomly. 3) Bad things trump good things. Despite my parents love of me and pride in my work and my own sense of having done well, the loss of Buffy permeated that day and the next few weeks so deeply that it was as if the award had never been given. The trophy vaporized out of existence. In our home, at that time, sadness and disappointment were easier to hold onto than joy.

Perhaps this is true for you as well. Perhaps your family did not know what I did not know for many years: that though we have little control over the frequency and intensity of sorrow in our lives, we do have control over one essential thing: ourselves, and how we respond to the unpredictability of our one tender life. In this moment we can choose how we hold the horror of life and its miraculousness. We can decide how long to stay devoted to sorrow and how often we attempt to ease that sorrow with what enlivens us. Terrible things do happen. Wonder does ascend. Both are true. Finding our way toward a life that thrives, even with great pain, requires that we acknowledge both truths and choose our response.

Think of Viktor Frankl ... concentration camp survivor, #119,104 ... three years in Theresienstadt, Auschwitz, Dachau, ... lost all but one family member. There was a moment, recorded here, when he actively, consciously chose to stop focusing on the small questions that haunted him — "How much will I have to eat today?" "Will the guard be cruel?" — and shift his focus to larger questions. He began to imagine himself standing in front of an audience of students, years later, lecturing them on how we survive the holocausts of our lives intact. While his every day unfolded as a living nightmare, within himself he began to create a refuge of hope, uplift and of possibility. He wrote, "I became disgusted with the state of affairs which compelled me, daily and hourly, to think of only such trivial things. I forced my thoughts to turn to another subject. Suddenly I saw myself standing on the platform of a well-lit, warm and pleasant lecture room. In front of me sat an attentive audience on comfortable upholstered seats. I was giving a lecture on the psychology of the concentration camp! All that oppressed me at that moment become objective, seen and described from the remote viewpoint of science. By this method I succeeded somehow in rising above the situation, above the suffering of the moment..." (Frankl, *Man's Search for Meaning*, 1959).

There is a way to rise with the suffering of a moment. We need only begin where we can, with the choice we have the most control over: who we will be in the moment we have been given. We need not be Frankl to make this shift. We are enough, as we are, to come to that state of rising in the face of the assaults of our days.

Dr. Frankl went on to offer us perhaps the most powerful psychological question of the 20th century: "Who am I in the presence of this?" Who will I or we choose to be in the face of violence or betrayal, loss or shock? Who can we become even as our pets die, our bodies fail, our work no longer holds a glow? What kind of woman or man am I, really, as I face these realities? Do I choose survival and then a reshaping of life?

The door to happiness after loss opens here, in this very first recognition of the fact that we have a choice and that within that choice lies freedom; irrespective of what has been sent our way.

Lost

One minute you are in a day like any other day. The next you are in hell. It's that fast. The phone rings. You hear, "Something has happened. You must come." And everything that you thought to be true is thrown into chaos. Your best friend is dead, your child has cancer, your home crushed by tornado. There are a thousand ways to be torpedoed by capricious circumstances and with each explosion we find ourselves taken out of the life we had been living and into foreign land. A client of mine, a father diagnosed with ALS, likened it to a concussion: "It's impossible to think clearly. None of the usual data points add up. You go into a shock and when you come out of that shock you still don't know who you are or what your life is going to be."

Life is altered, sometimes temporarily, sometimes permanently. And in this altering, we experience great emotions: grief, terror, fear, anxiety, anger, confusion and despair. The world no longer adds up to what we thought it would add up to and we no longer know exactly how to proceed, nor what to do with our feelings. Emotions rise and fall or we find ourselves numb, shut down. Our minds don't function properly. We put our cell phones in the refrigerator and then spend hours searching for them. We forget to feed the pets or even the children. The day I received the call announcing my brother's illness — stage four cancer — it took me three hours to drive the Massachusetts Turnpike, a drive that normally took two. I would be driving along sort of normally and then I'd see a road sign and it looked like alien dialect and I couldn't read the sign and I would become distressed and I'd have to pull over and remind myself where I was and what I was doing. "I am on the Pike. I am driving home. The road is straight. I've done this before." And then I could drive a bit farther.

In the state of those first waves of realization, some of us cannot move, we hide under the covers of our shock. Others go into overdrive, racing through a moment, somehow believing that doing anything is better than doing nothing in the presence of pain. We make a hundred calls or we become mute. We can't eat or we reach for the bottle. We scream or we find ourselves on our knees, not remembering how we fell to the ground of our kitchen floor. We hear ourselves chanting over and over, "Please, please,

please." We have come to the end of what we know and have been cast into a kingdom without rules, without guides, without sustenance. In those first few moments or hours or days, we are lost.

And that is okay. Because that is how it is. We are lost. We must face that reality.

There is nothing to do during the immediacy of those first moments except be disoriented. We aren't quite ready yet to recognize options or even understand, perhaps, that we have a choice. We are in a cave, without light. Wisdom is buried somewhere under the layers of suffering. "Everything is in my face and everything in my face is stone," wrote Rilke. "I can see no way out and no way through." This is how it is when tragedy strikes. There is seemingly no way beyond the pain. It is impossible to stand in our highest selves quite yet. There is only one task we must accomplish in these early hours of hell on earth. We must breathe. We must stay alive. For the sake of our own destiny and the care of those we love, we must stay alive. That is all.

"If you want to conquer the anxiety of life,
live in the moment, live in the breath."

~ Amit Ray

Breathe

I t sounds so simple, childlike even, to say "just breathe." You would think in the territory of suffering that our first best move might be something extraordinary, a momentous act, like "dial this number to directly reach the appropriate divine being," or "go immediately to a sanctuary where you will be bathed in lavender and fed smooth foods until you can think clearly."

And yet consider this: whenever we see a friend in distress or a child heaving with the pain of something having broken, the first words we utter are, "Okay, take a breath." We know something about what begins to heal us without truly knowing it. Breath is the essence of life. We breathe to stay alive, to nourish the cells and organs of our body, and we breathe as a gesture of hope. It is the doorway to the next moment, and from that the next possible future.

With each breath the tiniest amount of change has already begun. We find ourselves in a slightly new present and eventually, after perhaps ten breaths or a hundred, or after 17 hours of breathing through the shock and the pain, we can begin to do a bit more, we can begin to choose.

In my twenties, depressed after a painful breakup, all I wanted to do was self-medicate by sleeping all the time. I had been married right out of college, a binding that lasted less than three years and suddenly, at the age of 25, I had left a home for an apartment, a husband for an empty bed. Everything seemed unstable and uncertain. Had I known to choose breath instead of numbness I would have been able to awaken, get out of bed, and see the opportunities that might be already unfolding. My relationship to my suffering, to my daily existence and to my very sense of self would have been different if I had understood what Thich Nhat Han said, "Breath is the bridge which connects life to consciousness." I might have reached out more. I might have found a connection to another who also knew heartbreak. I would have been a bit more clear, instead stumbling like a three-legged homeless dog from scrap to scrap of affection.

With breath as our focus, we slow down, become aware, and then we can choose how to respond, rather than simply react.

Physically our breath is rejuvenating, feeding the body with life-giving oxygen. Emotionally, breath provides us with micro-experiences of calm. As we focus on breathing we create tiny islands of respite from the intensity of emotion and eventually feelings begin to settle. As we attend to breath, our cognitions begin to align themselves away from panic and terror or rage or despair and slowly, useful thoughts or questions begin to emerge: "Who can I lean on?" "What has helped me in the past?" "What do I need to learn now?" Those would have been really handy my 25th year.

With mindful breathing, too, we form a new relationship with ourselves. In shock or despair the tendency is to become reactive…to take action that is historically familiar whether or not it is helpful. With calming breath, we demonstrate self-care, and from that place we are more likely to move in a direction that is nourishing. Spiritually, with each inhale and exhale, we bring toward us a slight liberty, an openness to that which is and that which is larger than us. Mindful awareness of the breath indicates a "radical receptivity to life," to quote author Megan McDonough, and that moves us toward connection…with life, with ourselves, with those who have chosen the same in moments of anguish.

For you see, there is no easy way out of pain. No magic bullet exists, nor any charmed formula to protect us from suffering. The story is told of a woman, who after losing her only child, walked hundreds of miles to find the Buddha. Hearing of her trek and her loss, the Buddha met her on the road and the mother begged the holy man to bring her son back to life. He responded that he would consider her request if first she would do one task.

"Anything," she replied.

"You must travel for a year and find the house of no suffering." And so she did. She walked as she could, knocked on every door, asked to find the home without pain, the family without hurt, and you know how this ends, we all know how this ends, there is no house without suffering. In this we will never be alone.

Returning to the Buddha, she had little to say, only that she no longer needed to ask of him what she had asked before.

Life will come together, to paraphrase Buddhist nun Pema Chodron, and then it will fall apart. Breath is an anchor. With it we can remain present long enough for the next choice in our journey to unfold. It is the beginning of the journey into the darkness, which so beautifully-paradoxically-powerfully is the only way out of the darkness. Breath is our first crucial choice, connecting us to the lineage of those who have chosen life and it is direct evidence of our life force itself becoming invigorated again in micro-moments, here, right here in the body, right here, exactly where we are. We need be nowhere else.

Sit quietly now.

Let the rhythm of your breath become even.

Focus your mind on your breath.

Notice its rise and fall.

If you become distracted, simply notice, say "oh well," and return to breath.

Stay with breath a moment, perhaps three minutes and then perhaps four.

And know that each time you choose this one action ... this quieting down to breathe ... you are preparing yourself to see options unfolding in front of you, ones that will bring you closer to peace and away from harm.

Crazytown

For the first few months after my brother's death the formula had to be followed. In order for me to sleep I had to watch two episodes of LOST, back to back, take an Ativan along with either a Benadryl or an Ambien. If I watched only one episode, or failed to take two of the three medications, I would not sleep at all. Somehow this worked, and in those three months it was, in my mind anyway, the only way I could sleep. Any variation, I told myself, would lead to an entire night of tossing and then I would be not only be useless the next day, but dangerously ungrounded. I might forget something import-ant . . . like my children. If I slept I could carry on. Without it I was certain I would literally fall apart.

Each night, as I prepared my laptop, lined up my pills — medications of which I had had no prior experience — some part of me knew that I had gone to crazytown. Meditation rituals, yoga nidra, body relaxation techniques, and prayer, practices I had engaged in for more than two decades, disappeared from my repertoire. They held no power for me. Only those magic pills and those mind-twisting episodes of LOST, which felt so resonant with my current state, held the way through.

In states of despair we are not ourselves. We cannot locate the grounding patterns and beliefs that held us steady. Prior to loss, we knew who we were. After, we become something unbounded by structure, as if the struts of our scaffolding shatter overnight and our very bones lose form. Like sudden fog, this state of craziness, of nutty perception and thought and behavior, descends. We neither seek nor can we anticipate the ways in which misery will break us, nor can we prevent its appearance.

Consider Madonna Badger. Advertising agency owner living with her three girls in Connecticut. A normal mom living a normal life. Her parents visiting for Christmas, 2011, the house decorated, her girls tucked in, waiting for Santa. In the middle of the night, fire erupts. All three children and Madonna's parents die. In the weeks after her survival she spoke of the feeling of not being in her body, floating elsewhere without the ability to fend off any pain. She crossed between mania and suicidality, every aspect of her being uncovered, raw, cracked with grief. She could not locate herself firmly nor protect herself.

She moved beyond herself, agonized with torment.

She was/is not alone. There are circumstances in life that will bring any one of us to crazytown; no one is spared this possible trajectory.

Our very capacity to love is what leaves us vulnerable and yet it is our greatest strength. When crazytown hits, salvation can be found in those around us who see a bit more clearly than we, and who will volunteer to help. Our work, the path back to a sanity that includes acceptance of what we have lost, is to let that help in, or seek it directly. No one rises alone, so too, no one recovers alone. The path to a new sanity, one that makes sense considering what has been taken, is constructed by leaning literally and figuratively on the shoulder of another who cares and can present us with the tools to begin rebuilding.

Professionals can assist; I call these the credentialed experts, ones who have a particular expertise to guide us along the way. Our best friends may provide comfort and wisdom. Madonna credits her eventual return to sanity to a friend who offered her a home in Little Rock and a psychiatrist who promised her he could help her feel better in six weeks. To help her get through the first Christmas that followed her tragedy, another friend invited her to Thailand. With this friend's encouragement, Madonna chose to volunteer in an orphanage, gifting some of her own daughters' toys to the

Thai orphans. After offering the toys, adults came over to pray for Madonna, and she found herself encircled with care. "Little by little," she stated in a *New York Daily News* article, "I was getting my brain back online."

Sometimes, too, a complete stranger appears as a guide. Once on a New York City subway train I was riding, we plunged suddenly into darkness, the train trapped between stations. None of us knew what was happening. Kept in silence, uninformed and uncertain, 17 minutes passed, long enough for us all to be on edge. At the 18th minute the train rocked forward and pulled into its next station, only few hundred yards away. We began to breathe as a group and moved cautiously toward the exits, as if the very train itself had become alien. I waited my turn, got up to head out and at the threshold in front of the doors stood a young boy, a stranger of seven or eight. He turned to me abruptly, looked me dead on and said, "Sometimes it takes a while to find the joy." Then he left. I froze, wondering, "Did that really happen?" and saw confirmation on the faces of the others around me who had witnessed his sudden blessing. His words, unbidden and bald, remained with me as a grace. In my crazy time, they echoed in my head, even as I downed my pills and loaded up my laptop. I lived in darkness, I pursued sleep as a drug, and still, yet, I knew, that joy could rise. He had told me. I believed him and held on.

The words and choices of others who have suffered similarly often hold the highest promise of return for us. In psychological terms I call these the "non-credentialed experts," those whom life has struck in similar fashion and are a bit further along the path. In the months of intense mourning, the only folk who truly made sense to me were the ones who had also lost a beloved sibling. They understood my specific journey into crazytown — the need for those pills and those episodes. They comforted me, too, through my dark distortion that in losing John, I had somehow lost my past.

In my grief, not only did I not sleep easily, time itself became uncertain.

Before John died, I thought history was fixed. His death blurred the shore from which we siblings were launched. I knew who I was because we three (Joe, Maria, John) had been in it together, nurtured on one specific ground in one specific time and released from one certain dock. When I turned to look behind, the day life demanded I let John go, my past unmoored, floated as an island without anchor. I had to find the photos of our childhood; it became a compulsion. I would stare at them, trying to remember exactly how it felt to wear the bellbottoms of the '70s, Johnny next to me dressed in t-shirts, white socks, sneakers.

The pictures seemed false, untrue. Pain unsettled everything, even time.

I found I didn't believe in my own history. Did we really grow up together? Had his hand been in mine all those years? Did I make him up, that soft palm in mine on the way to school, morning after morning? Had any of it been real?

The only ones who could offer a solace I could trust through this disintegration and a line back to reality were those who, too, had had loss in this form. My therapist, Cathy, who had lost an older brother years before, would listen to my description of distorted reality and remind me that grief's power is dis-ordering. As Joan Didion explains in her book, *The Year of Magical Thinking*, written after the sudden heart attack of her husband, "We do not expect this shock to be obliterative, dislocating to both body and mind. We might expect that we will be prostrate, inconsolable, crazy with loss. We do not expect to be literally crazy, cool customers who believe their husband (dead) is about to return and will need his shoes."

We don't expect crazy. We cannot plan for it. We can, though, let others lead us through until we settle again into reality . . . at least enough to know that we are no longer quite as lost, and that a while from now, who knows when, some of this living will make some kind of sense.

True Hope

Hope is a place on the other side of the bridge that takes time to get to. This is what eight-year-old Asa M. told me when I asked him about hope in light of the fact that one of his best friends had been diagnosed with Duchenne Muscular Dystrophy, a fatal disease. Hope is a place to reach toward, not a feeling, and in some respects he is right. It infers movement toward optimism and a sense of sunniness, and yet there is a bridge that must be crossed — a traveling from what is to something on the other side. Really, though, what is a healthy hope or a true hope in the face of Duchenne or any other fatal diagnosis? To find the will to continue to breathe with any consciousness and to shape a life that thrums, there must be some evidence of the faintest hope. What is this hope ... this hope that will sustain us?

Jerome Groopman, professor of medicine at Massachusetts General Hospital, asked this very question. In his early years as a physician he noticed a tendency within himself and some of his colleagues — a shying away from stating the truth to patients, especially when that truth would be difficult to hear. To protect themselves from the suffering that voicing a difficult diagnosis might cause, doctors often spoke either too vaguely, too abruptly, or in terms of a softened reality. Recognizing that this pattern not only caused confusion but separated him from his patients, Groopman began to search for an understanding of true hope — a hope that is real, not false, and helpful. Over time he discovered a profound paradox: true hope exists when we face reality exactly as it is — however severe. We don't deny, negate, soften or overstate reality and at the same time we help the patient create a path to a slightly better future. This notion of a better future is significant. While cure may not be possible in medical terms, a path toward a better future may include finding peace, joy or companionship along the road toward death.

According to Groopman, the patient is the one to determine what this better future looks like; it is his job to introduce the concept while being honest about reality as it is.

What would a true hope look like for any of us now, in this very moment?

A young woman I know, recovering from multiple thoracic surgeries in her early twenties, found that the path over that bridge to a new normal could only be made as she focused on the micro-moments of positive healing that occurred each day. When the pain shifted from ten to 9.5, she imagined herself in an even better future the next day, down perhaps to 9.2, and then when reaching that milestone, she focused on a future that included a pain experience of only 8 and so on.

During the ten weeks my brother Johnny lived with disease, true hope had little to do with cure. Metastatic cancer, stage four, with significant symptoms in his pancreas, liver, and kidneys – this was the reality we faced. Hope for my brother lived in the chance to do right by his children, to prepare the documents he needed to in order to ensure his family would be set financially and to love while he could. The slightly better future, until the last agonizing weeks, had to do with relationships, inviting his fraternity brothers and colleagues and friends to remember what had been great about their time together. And at the center of this choice of hope for him was the daily opportunity to remind his four children of his love for them. One of John's last conscious acts was to order rings for them and his wife – each inscribed with a private message.

Reality required that he honor his own coming death, but until that very moment each day was also an opportunity to shape a future — the next hour, the next morning — such that they had meaning for him. This became his bridge.

When we deny reality we cannot make effective choices. We stumble about looking for a solution. Without a clear-headed acknowledgment of what is true, we make decisions that are only temporarily sustaining, or even harmful. Ignoring a diagnosis of melanoma, a patient of mine chose instead to move ahead with the launch of a business in Latin America, believing that if she ignored the cancerous mole, it might go away. A father I worked with refused to be tested despite escalating profound pain in his abdomen, thinking that if he admitted how much pain he was experiencing, his peers would think him weak. He nearly died from the rupturing of his appendix. As we pretend that what is true is not, we disempower ourselves from making wise choices.

And yet, scaffolding consisting only of reality cannot build hope. We need also a second set of framing girders and beams. We need the struts that bring a sense of a future that includes warmth, possibility, healing of a kind. As my mother-in-law, Frieda, came to the end of her days, fully aware that she had but a few weeks left, she took out her address book and began to call friends and relatives, taking the time to thank each of us for what we had brought to her life. True hope for her existed in the hearth of connection and the choice to say goodbye with both gratitude and dignity. There would be no cure, but there could be love.

Often we can't change reality. We can however change our experience of reality and open a door to a day that has a smidge more of what we truly wish for in it.

This bridge-building of hope does not happen immediately. It takes time to absorb dark news and time for our psyche to adjust enough to let go of what could have been to face what is, and then to consider what is possible in the presence of what is now true. For some time, we may not know what to hope for, but the knowledge that the practice of hope can be one of groundedness in reality and agency in creating days that offer uplift...well, that knowledge itself is a balm and an inspiration.

The Stories
We Tell Ourselves

Somewhere along the trajectory of my youth I picked up the habit of telling myself stories . . . except I didn't know I was doing so. I would think, "I'll never find love," after I had been rejected by a boy and think that that was somehow a true thought. Or in my twenties, in the midst of upheaval at work, I'd go to sleep at night believing that no one else in my generation felt this much worry, or carried this much self-doubt. I had a tale for everything and for the most part those tales were profoundly negative and limiting. Along the pathway of my youth I had come to believe beliefs, myths really, about what should be true and had a difficult time seeing that my life as it existed had its own truth and these myths I carried in my mind were falsehoods disguised as fact.

In the territory of loss, stories abound about how we should behave and what we ought to feel. Last week I received a call from a former student, asking for information about a resilience seminar because she found herself profoundly affected by the loss of her parents, three years after their deaths. In her mind, this was far too long to grieve, and the story she had begun to tell herself was that she was wrong, there was a timeframe to grief and she had far overrun its proper course.

Another patient of mine, a woman with stage two breast cancer, asked for a private consultation because she felt like she didn't belong in the cancer support group world. In her words, "My cancer is curable. How can I possibly whine about my fears or how I can't sleep at night if I'm next to someone with a much harder diagnosis? I should feel better about this, but I don't, so I just don't go." The myth she had stepped into was the myth that there is a hierarchy of pain and that you are only allowed to feel what you feel if you are in the top ten worst diagnoses or have had the top five worst losses. Parents who have lost one child will feel like they shouldn't complain in the presence of someone who has lost more than one. Teens with chronic illness feel ashamed of their anxieties when they meet a teen with a life-threatening diagnosis. The story we tell ourselves is that other people's pain trumps ours so therefore we need to shut down what we feel and carry on as if nothing has really happened and our suffering is really quite small.

This is one perspective I wish we could all live into: *Pain is pain is pain.* How it comes to us is not nearly as important as how it impacts us and what we choose to do with the opportunity to wrestle with its effects. We could use the pain of any loss, such as that of a beloved pet, to open our hearts and connect us to the reality of suffering everywhere, or we can dishonor our experience, judge it and ourselves, and put a wall around our hearts and lock others out and ourselves in.

And in terms of timing . . . well, grief has its own timeframe . . . and this is what I have come to understand: *there is no timeframe.* Grief rises, falls, dissipates, and then pins us once more like iron under a blacksmith's hammer. There is little predictability to the floods of sorrow, even years after a loss. The sound of summer baseball, now four years after Johnny's death, can send me to my knees with the memory of hours playing whiffle ball with the Hogan kids and other neighbors on our corner lot in upstate New York. There is no magic time in which grief finally disappears. Better to consider grief as a road, sometimes dense, dark, harsh, like through a wood, sometimes one of quicksand and swamp, and sometimes, a narrow trail, a rocky climb on the edge of a cliff that can be navigated only one small step at a time. And sometimes too, the journey of grieving can seem like the walk along the rim of the ocean, soft sand underneath, the pull of forces strong yet beautiful near us, and the sun shining anyway. There is no formula and there is no one experience of the road. Our anguish will exist as it is on its own terms.

A third knowing I wish for each of us: *It is not our fault.* We can become tortured with the belief that if only we had eaten more spinach or had spent more time expressing anger, we wouldn't have cancer today. If only we had not taken those four extra minutes to have one more cup of tea, our son, in another state, miraculously would not have stepped onto that road in the exact second the drunk driver careened around the corner. Or we imagine that if we had kept our daughter out of the pool as a child, she never would have jumped the quarry wall as a teen and broken her neck. We become caught in magical thinking that we could have rewritten the storyline and prevented life from having its way with us. And once in a while, perhaps, this is true. Perhaps choosing to eat only junk food for decades does eventually contribute to a diseased body...and yet more often than not, disease is multifactorial, tragedy is unpreventable, and accidents do happen. Moreover, blame is distracting and unhelpful. We come by our vulner-abilities and our fragile mortality honestly. There is no perfect here on the planet and none of us is godlike in our ability to know in advance what will result from the millions of micro-choices we make each day.

I'll say that again. *There is no perfect here on this planet.*

Life will have its way with us. Rather than spend time in a story of blame and shame, perhaps we can free ourselves a bit to consider this tale: we have little control. The control we do have sometimes isn't enough. As we learn to forgive ourselves for not being able to protect everyone we love in every way, including ourselves, we become a light that can offer that learning to others when they are struck. In this way our suffering begins to have a meaning that is larger than our particular experience. In this way we help others create a story that offers connection and warmth and moves them out of the prison of myths that truly are not true, that only serve to keep us cold and small.

Pain is pain is pain.

There is no perfect way to grieve or recover or rise.

We have little control over life.

We all mess up and life is a bit of a messpot.

We are simply human ... and that is okay.

"If you suddenly and unexpectedly feel joy,
don't hesitate. Give in to it."

~Mary Oliver

What We Feel

When my starter marriage failed (early 20s, right out of college, three years long, we should have just lived together for God's sake), I found myself in a profession I hated (public relations consultant for software companies) moving from apartment to apartment (four) in 18 months, shifting friendships with each move. For months I felt as though I walked around with a scarlet "D" on my chest. D for divorce, D for despair. Life, love, work, the Big Three, all of them a terrifying mystery to me. While my peers began to settle down and think about engagements, I had already crashed and burned through a marriage, home and career. I felt as though a tsunami had swept in and everyone else knew the secret to a great life, while somehow I had not gotten the memo. I woke every morning thinking, "I hate myself. I hate my life," and thought that was normal. I began to have feelings. Lots of them. I had no idea what to do with the terror or the despair. They were relentless, like hounds, and consuming.

Emotions cannot help but surge. I wish I had known that then. It is their nature and their gift. When we are crushed by life, we are often at the mercy of a heave of feelings and as they rise, they captivate us. Mistakenly, we come to believe that we are owned by them. Rage rockets us into impulsive action. Anguish devours us. We are swamped by sorrow or flooded with fear. We feel so very much and what we feel is often excruciating. Yet, also, almost unbelievably, the hopeful emotions, the possibilities of cure or reunion or resurrection, they arise too. Hours of sorrow are followed by buoyancy or the serenity of amity, of affection. Gratitude appears for the kindness of others. Emotions dance to a rhythm we seemingly cannot control or predict. And this we must allow to the best extent we can.

We must feel our feelings. Allow them to rise and fall, to enter into our awareness and flow through us and to then dissipate in their own time. At our healthiest this is what happens. Emotions remain in motion, moving in and moving out, shifting as the day edges forward. Allowing them to flow, we come to find the truth of our experience. Here's Anne Lamott:

"But you can't get to any of these truths by sitting in a field smiling beatifically, avoiding your anger and damage and grief. Your anger and damage and grief are the way to the truth. We don't have much truth to express unless we have gone into those rooms and closets and woods and abysses that we were told not go in to. When we have gone in and looked around for a long while, just breathing and finally taking it in — then we will be able to speak in our own voice and to stay in the present moment. And that moment is home."

We mustn't negate that we are afraid or angry or disheartened, nor that we feel hopeful or optimistic. Instead we must allow ourselves to know what we truly feel and invite ourselves to become comfortable there, comfortable with the good, at ease with the difficult. We can only make wise choices about how to respond when we allow our authentic experience first. It would be senseless to try to be happy while we are actively terrified and insanity-making to pretend to only be sad or only be worried or only be happy. Have you met that person? The one who is always smiling and everything is fine and her shoes match her bag or his tie aligns perfectly with the oh-so-perfect cinch of his jacket every single day? Or the one who can never admit that she is content or inspired or optimistic? Frankly, it's exhausting to be near them . . . almost as exhausting to be them, to force ourselves to feel what we don't feel.

Can we lay that burden down?

As we let our feelings simply be, they catalyze the rising of other emotions, other possibilities. Sorrow, when fully experienced, often opens into sweetness or humor, anger transforms into compassion, tenderness becomes fear for the vulnerability of others, which then becomes kindness. As we allow ourselves to feel one aspect of loss, our capacity to experience the full range of emotions available to us increases. Israeli Prime Minister Golda Meir once wrote, "Those who don't know how to weep with their whole heart don't know how to laugh either." And the opposite is true. Each time we make room for the fullness of our joy and delight, we create a reservoir within ourselves that enables a greater safety in which to experience regret, torment, and terror. Emotions no longer hold us captive, locking us into a too-narrow way of being. Our emotional capacity becomes wide and deep, fluid and flexible.

When that happens we can see, really see.

The Gift of Sight

The morning my brother died the air was lit with spring. The North Carolina dogwoods boasted half-open buds and the sun was warm enough for kids to go to school in shorts and tank tops. I remember the light, the passing of clouds around and over the rooftops. It was maybe supposed to rain. My brother was maybe supposed to live a week or so. His daughter Juliana was home, and son James was in school for the morning, and his oldest daughter, Rosemary, had flown back to college to take mid-terms and would return in a day or two. David, his oldest boy, was home in the house with us. It was a Monday. The hospice nurse sat to the right of my brother, checking his vitals, and on his left an energy healer, Sharon, was laying hands on him, whispering, "Peace, peace, peace." The nurse suddenly signaled me; it was time. Within moments my brother's wife, Sheila, her siblings, David and Juliana, my parents, me and my older brother, Joe, all found our own words to tell John we loved him and let him know it was okay to go. He passed within minutes. We did not have a week, it turned out, and now we had not even a second left.

Someone ran the quarter mile to gather James from school. Someone called Rosemary at college, and somehow my brother's ER colleagues got the news and began to arrive. It became so close inside, so dense with sorrow that I moved outside. I stood on the porch and remember thinking, "This is what shock is, this is what shock feels like." I could stand and breathe and see and yet my feelings swirled. I would sob, then be calm, my body would heave and then become weightless, untethered. I noticed the clouds had gone, the threat of rain passed. My stomach hurt horribly, and yet my skin felt alive, awakened. I watched the light become pink, the pink of pearl, of opal, stared as it caressed the stone walkway. Mid-morning sun cut across the driveway, shadow, then light, darkness, then bright, my mind mesmerized by the shifting pattern. I could hear my heart pound in my chest, and I would panic at its bang and then it would still. It felt as though everything was happening at once within me ... aching and awareness, upheaval and calm, shock and clarity. It all moved in a churning loop and then I heard a sound. A new sound.

I looked up. From down the asphalt street, children arrived. I heard the shuffle of sandals and the tread of Nikes. Teenagers from the school my brother's children attended walked in pairs, groups of three. They had left their classes. Without backpack or lunch, without hall pass or permission slip they came. Twelve-year-olds and seniors. The girls from soccer and the boys from band. Two, then five, then thirteen, and then so many I could not count. They walked up the drive, passed me on the porch and without hesitation entered my brother's home to find their friends, my nieces and nephews. I wondered for a second about what the head of school must be thinking and then thought what I thought what those kids must be thinking, "Fuck school, this is way more important."

"We can do no great things," Mother Theresa once said, "only small things with great love." Small things trod the curve of John's walkway, up the five steps through his doorway, touched the tile of his foyer and moved up the staircase to his children's bedrooms. Great love entered my brother's home, wearing shorts and jeans.

As we allow ourselves to feel, we allow ourselves to see, to open to wonder that is present even as the shatterings occur within us and around us. We become part of the dance with life, not separate from any of it, nor split from any aspect of ourselves. We permit feeling and from this we inhabit our very being — inhabit, from the Latin habeo, meaning to have, and habitare, meaning to live or to dwell. We dwell in ourselves as we are — full of pain and awareness, attuned to our agony and that of others, the body contorted and awake. We are home within ourselves as our lives fracture.

This inhabiting doesn't require the presence of others, it requires our presence within ourselves — as we feel, we see, and in our seeing we are freed.

We come to understand in that moment that some aspect of heaven exists in hell, even as we are breaking.

"One had to take some action against fear
when once it laid hold of one."

~ *Ranier Marie Rilke*

Facing Fear

There is so much we fear in life. We dread change, we are trepidatious about failure. Some of us worry about success, about becoming too large, too bright or never becoming ... X. We are worried about failing health, afraid of accidents, and at some, often unconscious level, we are apprehensive about not getting it all right ... as if the secret to a happy life was a formula with exact requirements and after having fulfilled those requirements we would be THERE!! ... that place where all is well and nothing bad ever happens. Many of us lived into that formula in our twenties as if the right car, the right makeup, the right job, the right guy, and knowing the right club or film or party to attend would somehow keep the dragons of not-fitting-in at bay and we would suddenly love ourselves and be okay.

Fear rules us often. And then something bad does, in fact, happen. Something we've dreaded or didn't even know to fear happens and we wake to find ourselves dazed and bloodied, suddenly uncertain of everything. I remember learning once of a jogger who, on a well-used running trail in the hills behind her home in Oregon, was mauled and killed by a mountain lion. How the hell do we plan for that? How do we possibly ever protect against that? Life attacks and a new fear may ascend then, one primitive and destabilizing . . . the type of fear that inspires one to stay in the cave of one's bed and simply refuse to face the day. We fear that once having been struck by the gods we are marked as a perpetual target. We have been made vulnerable, and at any one moment an arrow will strike again, and we will fall, again.

In May, 2001, Koby Mandell and his best friend, Yosef, skipped school for a day, something they had never done before, to play in the caves of Tekoa, Israel, hidden in a canyon 100 yards from his home. Koby had turned 13 that year, the oldest of the four children of Sherri and Seth Mandell. His mom describes him as shy outside the house but with a passion for telling jokes. Lively in school, he followed American sports and he and Yosef were known to talk for hours. The past tense is important here because on that late spring day Koby and his best friend were murdered, their bodies bludgeoned to death by terrorists with rocks.

Twelve years after Sherri lost her son, I met her for dinner. Over the course of that meal we discussed how her younger children, now in young adulthood were faring and she said the following, "It's been hard for them lately. They've lost other people. A friend's dad to a heart attack. Another friend to a bomb." She paused for a moment. "It's hard when your children figure out that one loss is not the only loss they will face." I sat silent, struck by the simplicity of her statement. Our losses are not protective; one great big horrible tragedy does not insure us against others. We can slip into magical thinking that because our father died when we were 12 or our mother became an addict when we left for college, somehow that is "enough" and it wouldn't be fair of life to hit us hard a second or a third time, not fair at all really, and there must be a just balancer somewhere who is keeping track of these sorts of things. Yet, there is no such balancer, no even accord. We are neither marked by life, nor immunized. Life is life. She is capricious and will have her way with us irrespective of our magical thoughts, or our perfect formulaic life, or the talismans we wear around our necks.

Death, to paraphrase the poet Michael Ryan, rises like a dinosaur out of a duck pond as it will, so, too, disease, injustice, famine and fire. Rightly so, we are afraid.

What to do then? Once terror roots in our bones and we notice how our bodies have responded with sweat or headache or trembling, what is our choice? What engenders resilience? How do we free ourselves from its tyranny?

One has to take action, confirms Rilke. Nothing grows in states of fear. This we know.

Antidotes to fear abound in the psychological and medical literature: Connection to others soothes us and also inspires bravery. Wisdom from those who have traveled similar paths provides us light and clarity. Mindful awareness of the flow of emotions enables us to find a tiny bit of space between one moment of fear and another, eventually creating islands of calm within. Laughter ameliorates life's sharp edges, and forgiveness, generosity, and gratitude create positive neurochemical adjustments within the brain that generate room for hope, optimism, and a sense of self-agency. In their presence we can begin to feel, however slightly, a growing sense of competency in facing horror. There is much we can do. Each of these strategies rests first though on a simple foundation: we must first accept that we are afraid and offer ourselves a tender self-compassion for finding ourselves hidden under the covers, certain of the velociraptor under the bed.

When fear arises the freeing action, the resilient action, the profoundly difficult action, is neither to override nor deny fear, but to turn and face it, directly, as one might turn to face a snarling slayer.

We do so not to let the creature overcome us, but rather to see, to see clearly, that which might paralyze us. As we do, we can find that perception shifts. Facing fear, naming it out loud, stating where it lives in our body, what the paralysis really feels like, reduces some of its power. What had appeared as a predator suddenly, with our direct attention, becomes more like a messenger or guide.

Pema Chodron writes of a childhood friend, terrorized by nightmares of monsters. She asked her friend what the monsters looked like, and the girl realized she didn't know. Soon in her dreams she saw herself turning to face the demons in order to see them clearly and as she did they became approachable and even friendly. The nightmares became dreams, the monsters became companions.

With clear seeing, other knowings arise; perhaps the knowing that we have walked with this fear for a very long time or that along with fear we also possess tenacity, bravery, curiosity. Wonder may grow at how often we have been captivated by our fear. Courage, a defiant sense of "damn it, I am not going to let this imprison me," will show itself for some. And self-compassion may grow, a poignant humility for the ways in which we are simply human and vulnerable to the reality that we have control over so little. Our very smallness may remind us to be tender toward ourselves.

As we turn to face fear, our vision of the worst shifts and our heart calms. We can bring ourselves back to the present moment where choice abounds and let go of the terror of what might yet be or what has been and attend to the moment that is. "Fear keeps us focused on the past or worried about the future," counsels Thich Nhat Han. "If we can acknowledge our fear, we can realize that right now we are okay. Right now, today, we are still alive, and our bodies are working marvelously. Our eyes can still see the beautiful sky. Our ears can still hear the voices of our loved ones."

In the presence of the present moment, fear can become one of the many experiences of living; not the predominant experience, not the one that need define our life.

"Use your life to illuminate something larger."

~ *Phyllis Theroux*

Why Me?

A colleague asked me an unusual question last week, "What do I do with the guilt of having done so well when the rest of my family struggles?" He referred to "doing well" as financial security and a stable, healthy family, but he could have been speaking to any number of the elements of guilt present in us when life treats us well: better homes, healthier bodies, less illness, less struggle, less dying. And in a funky way, his question felt like the flip side of a question I am asked far more often: "Why me? Why this much suffering?" I suggested to my friend the same thing I have suggested to those who become caught in the 'why me' whirlpool; both questions, I responded, come from the wrong end of inquiry.

The "wrong end" are those questions that lead us into closed alleys, separating us from the wholeness of life and others. They stand in contrast to questions that expand and enhance our humanity, and bring us to a place of largeness within ourselves. Whether we are in pain and or in states of joy, we ought be looking for the questions that enliven us and bring us to a place of resonance with life itself. We ought to attempt to quiet any questions, however normal and natural they are, that keep us believing that we are special and therefore distinct and lead to a splitting away from others. "Why me?" either as a query about why so much torment has come my way, or why so much goodness has come my way, tends to inherently keep us apart.

I prefer a different inquiry.

I have come to favor thinking that grounds and soothes me, lifting me while honoring both the depth of my pain and the breadth of abundance that has appeared.

For now at least, I've buried the "Why me?" question right next to "How come?" and "What's the point?" Let the dogs dig for them or the weasels hunt for the slight marrow in their bones. I have found them an unsatisfactory gnawing; a meager meal. I turn instead to the thinking of the wisdom traditions of the east and the Tibetan Bon reflections on the nature of suffering and abundance, thinking that orders itself like this:

Suffering is.

Abundance is.

When, why and how they appear is mostly a mystery.

They simply are.

Better to focus on how we receive them and what we do with them, than on why they showed up in the first place.

We are back to choice then, and the notion that a part of what comes our way is ours to craft, to shape, to mold in some way . . . either toward the benefit of ourselves and others . . . or not. We might, the Tibetans suggest, hold our suffering as if it were precious, for in recognizing our pain we are given the opportunity to grow into compassion for the pain of others. We might then, too, hold the goodness and abundance that has come our way as precious, for as we do so, we model for others the opportunity to savor that which is good. And, too, so that we may be full and nourished when misery appears another time; which it will unpredictably, capriciously, and certainly.

None of these grand perspectives may be evident at first or easy to hold onto. "In the hot pit," says author Janet Elsbach, "I am not thinking broadly or generously, at least for a time." Yet knowing of this possibility, having the language for a larger way of seeing can in and of itself trigger a shift of attention away from the 'me' inherent in "Why me?" and toward the 'us' inherent in "How do I use this well?"

Even this great goodness, we might find ourselves saying, I allow in and offer back to the world for the benefit of myself and others.

Even this pain, we might consider thinking, I recognize — from *cognere* — to know or to know again — so that I might be softened toward compassion for others.

Whiplash

It's a normal day. We are going along fine, getting done what needs getting done, the shopping, the bills, the movement of piles from one spot in the house to another. In my daily life I have piles of clothes to give away, piles of old magazines I might want to go through, piles of small branches near the wood stove, in case a freeze might come in the midst of June. My piles define me and ground me in an ironic sort of way. As long as I have piles to sort I am familiar to myself and have something to do when life hits one of those boring patches.

I am not alone here. Days can be like this. Normal. Regular. A little dull. Piles piled up. We move toward a stack to get a job done, to fill a little time, and then a song floats from a radio or the scent of lilac drifts through the screen door and suddenly we are jolted, slammed back into pain. The heart hits hard against the cage of the loss we thought we had somehow 'resolved' and we find ourselves on our knees, paralyzed on the blue kitchen tile, staring at the Tupperware we had taken out of the drawer to sort...and we can't remember why because we can't breathe, can't hold our head up, can't possibly organize anything because all we can feel is this rush of pain and the pressing crush of its sensation. As if we have been t-boned by a Hummer. Whiplash and slam.

Our minds tell us this can't or shouldn't be happening. After all, it's been weeks, months, years. Our ego tells us to hide this, don't call, don't tell because who wants to hear about our pain so long after the 'legitimate' time to grieve has passed? We feel embarrassed or shamed or confused. We are supposed to finish this chore and head on to the next but we can't possibly move. Our heads drop to the floor, supplicant now to the hurt, and we feel the sobs rising, and we cannot believe it can feel this bad so long after the original blow.

A father I know, married 23 years, with nearly-grown children, called me one afternoon to ask if perhaps I could help him get medication because five years after the loss of his wife he still hurts on certain days and does not want to feel it any more. He judges himself, "Shouldn't I be over this?" he asks and then becomes angry "How can this possibly be happening still? Enough!!" He begins to cry softly on the phone, apologizing for bothering me with this, but not knowing where else to turn. And then he says the thing many of us feel: "I want this to be over. I want to have moved on. I don't want to not love my wife but she's dead and I don't want to be married to a ghost anymore. I don't want to be hijacked by our love anymore."

We want the pain to stop. To be done. We have a new life now. Let the old one die.

This is true for some.

For others this:

A song triggers a crash. We are on our knees. We let the wave come and for a time all we want is to be back in time, our son on our lap, giggling at the sound of our puppy. This is years before the hurt, centuries before we knew boys could be taken so fast with such brutality. The pain curtains us into a trance; we are no longer in our kitchen. We are in the old house, with the yellow blankey around our son's shoulder and he smells like powder and we never ever want to leave that moment. The present loses its hold and we welcome the pain and the craziness because, at least for the duration of that swirling, crashing, time-bending lash, we are with him.

The pain makes him real. We want that real, not the one right in front of us. And the agony is not in our hurt; it's in the fading of the hurt. Let the new life disappear. For one completely irrational long stretch we jones for what was and mainline the pain in order to be back there. We stay on the floor of the kitchen for hours, pulling the threads of the past, even though each one slices and later someone much clearer will have to help us bind the wounds, again.

There is no rhyme to grief. No perfect rhythm that sets the path clear and certain. Grief is a jazz tune, not a minuet. It is an edge-searing drive up the Himalayas, not a Sunday cruise to the park. It will bring us to the ledge of sanity and show us the chasm, even though we have done all the proper work, even though we have crafted a new living, even though we are much much older. This simply is its nature. It is wild, unpredictable, a force untamable except through one posture, one response: face it. To witness as it comes, to watch ourselves be brought down and to love ourselves anyway; to recognize that, like love, grief's energy for a time will be larger than we are; to see and understand this, saying, "it's okay, we are outmatched, for now;" to remember that we never have to be in its fierce press alone; nor seduced or disgusted by its sudden arrival; and as it fades to cherish the one deep searing truth whiplash brings: we don't have time to waste not loving those we love.

"I wish I could show you when you are lonely or in darkness the astonishing light of your own being."

~ Hafiz

Loneliness

Two years ago, I found myself in a time of lessening connections. My daughter ensconced in college. My son, in high school, turning definitively and appropriately toward his peer group. My work travel increased making it more difficult to see my friends and my friend group shrank as some began to choose to move to new towns or return to where they had grown up. I had begun to date but that was a bare, depressing landscape. And I found myself either crazy busy with work or home alone with large pockets of empty time.

I don't love loneliness. Okay, that is a serious understatement. I have hated that feeling. I have battled its press ever since I can remember. As a child, being alone made me feel scared and wrong — like it was somehow my fault that no one wanted to play with me. As a college student I despaired against having

Friday nights with nothing to do; I remember feeling ashamed on those nights, so much so that I would turn my lights off so that no one would see that I had no plans. I would hide in my room, afraid to be known as the forlorn girl. In my twenties I fought hard against those moments by filling every free second with something to do, some place to be. It was grueling...but the exhaustion was better than the emptiness.

I wish I knew then that we all battle with this...and we all find ways to hide this from others. We over-schedule so we don't have to face the quiet. We stay in unhealthy marriages too long so that at least we have things to do. We fill our nights with work, our days with people we don't necessarily like to avoid the vulnerability, the raw nakedness of being without companionship. We pretend that Facebook offers community and we tweet just to know that someone is out there, someone may be listening.

Life, too, has its way with us and can force us into empty space and empty time. We do our best to make friends, engage in good work, learn new things, yet sometimes, despite our deepest efforts, relationships fade and communities change; we become isolated, stranded. It once took me so long to find friends after I had moved to a new town that I used to cry in the Price Chopper parking lot whenever I went to buy food. Something about seeing so many others on their way through the aisles with their carts, ensconced in what I assumed to be their perfectly happy lives — buying food for family meals or friendly dinners — only made my isolation worse. It seemed as if they had all been invited to a party, and I had not, and would not ever be.

As I aged, and found that loneliness continued to haunt me, I began to study what others had to say. Dag Hammarskjold, former Secretary-General of the UN, once wrote, "Pray that your loneliness may spur you into finding something to live for, great enough to die for," which seemed lovely, so big-hearted, so right and so damn impossible when seclusion swirled like fog. Philosopher and theologian Paul Tillich encouraged a shift of perspective, "Loneliness expresses the pain of being alone and solitude expresses the glory of being alone," and at times I attempted to reframe those long weekend nights as solitude, as an active choosing of connection with the privacy of my own being. Once in a while that would help for a few moments — until the sound of my own breathing, suddenly loud and unmet, simply became another indicator of the cavern of my life.

As those nights increased and my awareness of the fear of loneliness sharpened, I realized that I would rather be in pain than lonely. Pain, grief, worry, all brought with them some experience of feeling alive in my body and somehow connected to life, whereas loneliness felt deadening, as if I were in danger of fading away and no one would know or care. And despite the fact that this simply was not true — I had children, I had colleagues, I had friends — it felt true in moments, really, deeply true and possible that I had been utterly abandoned.

Where is life, when our experience of life is isolation? Where does hope reside? Or happiness?

I knew all the advice: Keep busy. Do what you love. Join clubs. Call someone, anyone, don't be picky. Meditate. Remember that it's probably temporary. Face the lonely places inside and see what it has to teach you. And I did all of this. On certain occasions it worked and the evening swung toward a sense of uplift. On other nights nothing worked and the spaciousness around me felt searing.

For me, I have come to realize, it is often quite hard to be lonely . . . harder than any other experience I have come to know so far.

One knowing has begun to shift my experience.

A girl I worked with, a teen, had only a few days left to her life. Her friends had left her because she had been in hospital so long. Her mother was dead. Her siblings had disconnected and her father lay dying as well of a brain tumor — a tumor that left him without the ability to remember that he even had a daughter. This teen would die in the presence of a hospice nurse and a distant relative who had flown in to care for her at the last moment. Essentially, she would die alone.

In her last few days of care in the hospital she begged me for one thing: to be remembered. She knew we would medicate her pain; this did not consume her. She did not ask for some sudden cure or promise of a heaven nor did she plead to us to keep her in the hospital. She had readied herself to die. Her deepest longing was to know she had mattered to us, that she would somehow continue to be known.

I promised her I would not forget her.

Now, in the most severe moments of my lonesomeness, when all else fails to provide ease, she will come to mind. I remember that she no longer has a chance to live into this living and she is missing so much: dragonflies over a pond as winter disappears, the colors of violet phlox and poppy orange, Canadian geese heading home over the northeast and the cry of coyotes, haunting our hills. There is so much life here that she cannot and will not ever know, that sweet sticky sigh after sex and the call of a friend who starts every conversation with "Hello there!" as if she has discovered you just now for the first time. She'll not know what it is like to race to the ER with a child allergic to bees, shoving Benadryl in her mouth, nor the ache of watching your son line up for the last shot in the last moment of the big game, knowing he will carry that moment with him the rest of his life, for better or worse. And she won't hold in her heart the wrap of pain, the tableau, the slow-motion ribbon of undoing as you turn your bike onto a busy road and see a tiny chipmunk in the opposite lane, trapped by a paw smashed by a car ... one paw glued to the ground ... her body wrenching away, her head bowing to the tarmac, and in that one second of seeing, that one moment of recognition you come to understand that you will be the last one to see her alive as you hear the car speeding directly toward her in that lane and there is nothing to do but watch or look away — it won't matter — her death clear whether you see it or not.

When all else fails, I remember her, this 17-year-old who died alone and somehow my loneliness becomes not the mark of my unworthiness, nor a prison in my life, but a place, at last, of connection. If I can do nothing else in the presence of the empty space and unfilled time that rests heavily, I can at least remember that while living I have a chance to experience so much more than she will ever have.

I have, at least, one day more to reach toward this life I have been given.

"No one saves us but ourselves."

~ Buddha

Where the Hell is That White Horse?

I don't want to die not having lived.

I wrote that sentence in my graduate school application essay for entrance into a clinical psychology doctoral program at the age of 28. Working in public relations for three years had just about poisoned my soul and I so longed for a new life, a new way of being in life that would energize me and help me feel I had a place in this world where the sun might shine.

A few years later, in the midst of my graduate training, friends and I sat around talking about why we had chosen psychology and I quoted this line from my essay. One friend suggested that if I really wanted to live I ought to stop looking for the white

horse. Her words landed hard that day, and per-
fectly, as a mallet might shatter a casing. A world of
assumptions began to break.

Victimhood and martyrdom had been the muddy
ground in which I had grown ... and their conse-
quent suppositions were the surround of my being:
I could only find my way out of the swamp of my
unhappy, difficult, burdensome life if someone on
a white horse rode up to the edge, threw me a rope,
and pulled me out. A large part of me existed as
a sleeping girl ... waiting, waiting, longing for the
right kiss, the perfect prince, the rescue in the night
and the sweeping journey into another land far
away. Author Phyllis Theroux describes that same
journey: "For so many years, more than half my life,
I struggled with the emotional belief that if I could
rest secure in the love of a partner I would blossom
like a flower well and truly planted. The idea that I
had soil of my own took a long time to mature."

Many relate to this. A new sorrow triggers a cascading
downward descent into the swamp of despair where
our lack of self-regard hold us in a near-drowning
state. "I can't do this myself." "Why does this always
happen to me?" "Everything bad that could happen
comes to me!" "God has it in for me." "I am being
punished." As these roots wrap around us, their
familiar hold prompts feelings of despair, disgust, a
quaking vulnerability, and sometimes hopelessness.
We belong in the swamp. We smell like swamp. We

will never get out of the swamp unless someone comes along to carry us out. We pray or at the least wait for the love that will change everything, or the friend who will heal all wounds, or the angels and spirit guides who will clean up our aura with crystalline bursts of light.

And under those beliefs, for some of us, exists a core terror: we are the swamp. Even if that magical prince or princess should appear...we will bring the swamp with us. Its stink will not leave us. We are destined, in other words, for misery. As a woman in one of my classes said, "Everything bad happens to me because I deserve it; I just don't deserve the happy shit. The bad shit is mine and I somehow have become comfortable in my misery even while I keep waiting for some relationship to rescue me."

The bad shit is mine. I am the swamp. Someone please rescue me. Where the hell is that white horse?

This is the point at which I often tell my students that I'm going to save them thousands of dollars in therapy...thousands that I myself spent on my quest for rescue. There is no white horse, there is no rescue except that which we offer ourselves. Let me repeat that. *There is no rescue except by ourselves for ourselves.* Once we begin to hold this thought as a possibility — that the most firm sustaining rope out of the swamp emanates from within — then true rescue is possible. Rescue that offers firm footing, calmness, clarity of thought and heart, even when the tragic comes our way again. The Buddha understood this centuries ago: "No one saves us but ourselves. No one can and no one may. We ourselves must walk the path."

What does that look like?

It looks like a woman, every day, bringing a bit more self-compassion to her days by repeating once a day, "I am beginning to like myself."

Or a man, choosing each night to spend a few moments with his guitar, because he loves the feel of his hands against the guitar, he loves what it reminds him of from his past, and he needs, in a soul-drinking way, the nourishment of sound.

It looks like the grandmother, for the first time in her life, choosing to show up for a community volunteer group to knit shawls for the ill, instead of drinking herself to sleep each night.

And it looks like this: a 31-year old, hearing her friend tell her to stop looking for a white horse, asking everyone she trusted how they did just that, and borrowing their ideas until she could come up with her own. I did not know what life felt like as a non-victim but I knew that others knew and I began my own journey of swamp-rising by stealing good ideas from those ahead of me on the path. "I am the one I've been waiting for," became my mantra and my prayer and I chose each day to do something that signaled to me that I was an agent in my own life. My initial act of self-rescue, which I practiced for months, became a daily meditation in which I imagined my younger self, at the age of 3, held her in my arms, told her I would not abandon her and invited her to join me in living with greater courage. I carried her with me in my heart each day until I began to know, to really deeply know, that in rescuing her from isolation I had climbed onto more stable ground and from that place could begin to walk toward my own life.

> *"Everyone must come out of his exile in his own way."*
>
> ~Martin Buber

Exile

Exile: from the Old French "essillier," to banish, expel, drive off, cousin to the Greek "alaomai," to wander or stray. Stories abound in the wisdom literature of figures leaving their homes, wandering by choice in order to know a new reality. Siddhartha walking away from the fortress of his royal life; Shams, eventual teacher of the poet Rumi, leaving his family to journey in search of the object of his divine longing; Jesus wrestling forty days and nights in that bloody desert; Mirabai, rejecting the traditions of her esteemed family to travel the whole of northern India, composing song and poetry, dancing in honor of her beloved, Lord Krishna. So many leavings, to find what is true within, requiring a journey away from that which has been and a shirking of bonds that do not serve.

This choosing of distant places and other peoples is a self-induced exile, an invitation to the self and a preference. But the exile that appears in the territory of loss is not this choosing ... it is a forced expulsion from the familiar into a land unbidden and unwanted.

My friend, Scotty, lost his home and all his belongings to fire. I visited him a few weeks later with odds and ends to fill his new apartment. I asked him about this possible new beginning and I won't ever forget the look on his face ... one of disbelief that I had suggested anything positive about this experience. "I've got to start all over again. I've lost my photos, my music, clothes ... everything. You can't imagine how dislocated I feel." Clearly I couldn't, and in my naiveté I had only exacerbated his pain at being dumped into a desert not of his choosing. The walk back to a sense of comfort, of home, would be, for the most part, a solitary walk. We could bring him things; but only he could create home within. That would take longer than the 14 days I had given him.

What to understand then when exile is forced?

People often kindly ask me how my brother's children are doing and I usually reply with the standard set of responses. By all outward appearances Johnny's children are well: they have friends, they've continued in school, they play sports, work out, listen to music, celebrate their birthdays and in general take care of their bodies and their minds. But I have no idea, really, how they are doing in terms of crossing through the ocean of grief. Each stroke they take forces them away from what had been toward a land they didn't select and would never choose to belong to. I wonder about the cost of feeling different than their peers, of not belonging to what had been a 'normal' living any longer.

In those years after my first divorce, walking the streets of Boston with that scarlet D on my chest, I experienced exile from my peer group. I walked the same streets, worked the same job, bought tea at the same cafes, hung out with the same friends and yet I felt foreign and displaced, as if I had arrived as an immigrant without papers and not quite understanding the language. For months, I felt ill. Sick to my stomach, and also in my heart, as if the organ itself were failing and could not send proper blood flow to keep me going. Walking seemed a difficult task, and running, an act of courage. Nothing worked well.

Here is Brene Brown on this need to fit in, to know one's place, to belong to another: "A deep sense of love and belonging is an irreducible need of all people. We are biologically, cognitively, physically, and spiritually wired to love, to be loved and to belong. When those needs are not met, we don't function as we were meant to. We break. We fall apart. We numb. We ache. We hurt others. We get sick."

When fire consumes the structure of our lives, when outcast from work or love or the familiar, we don't do well and we often feel alone in the not doing well. No one else can truly know our experience. This is the penumbra of exile. In forced solitude we feel banished from a sustaining tie. We long to belong and do not.

Our new home . . . the one we might uncover if we keep our eyes and our hearts open . . . exists with those similarly banished.

For months after John's death, the only folk I felt truly connected to or safe with were those who had lost a sibling. With them, I felt a kinship and an 'okayness' not present for me anywhere else. One of the first suggestions I make to parents who have a child living through extended medical treatment is to help them find other children or teens who are also losing hair, or missing a limb or suffering the indignities of scar tissue on a body that had been innocent. With those like-wounded others, children find comradeship and a sense of not being quite so 'other.'

Elizabeth McCracken, in her work, *An Exact Replica of a Figment of My Imagination*, composed after the stillborn birth of her first child, wrote of finding her people in those she came to meet who were also forced to deliver a child who had died in utero. "All I can say is, it's a sort of kinship, as though there is a family tree of grief. On this branch, the lost children, on this the suicide parents, there the beloved mentally ill siblings. When something terrible happens, you discover all of a sudden that you have a new set of relatives, people with whom you can speak in the shorthand of cousins."

It might have been wiser to have shown up to Scotty's apartment with new towels and the number of one other person whose life had also been torched by fire. They may not have made the same meaning out of the fire, may not have found the exact same way back into the architecture of their lives, but they certainly would have shared a shorthand of experience that would have helped them navigate a path back to wholeness.

The Art of Losing

Without a white horse or a potion to spare us from eruptions and agonies we are left with having to face a truth of living that many do not bear well. Much of life is about a falling apart, a losing of what had been. Our schools, teams, parents counsel us to win, achieve, strive for the best and there is much merit here — without such intention we might fail to find our way toward our best lives. And yet we must also uncover within us an aptitude for the art of losing, for there is no striving without defeat and there is no living without loss. This is as certain as night follows day and any movement toward a happier, more whole existence occurs most healthfully and easefully when we understand how to shape a life around loss, just as we choose to shape a life around striving for excellence.

Not long ago I met with a family of four children and a dad. Their mother, in her mid-30s, lost her life to cancer. The oldest child was nine, the youngest was three. I did not tell the dad that the two little ones would not remember their mom except in the most general sense, but I did let him know that this loss has shaped the path of their lives as few others will; it will influence their choices, definitively, for decades. I assessed how our community might best support them, what they most needed to manage the acute pain, and because the dad asked for the barest, darkest of truths, he and I had an excruciating conversation, one in which I told him he would never know how to do this perfectly, nor could he completely find a way to protect his children from further loss; they were suffering and they will suffer, and we could not yet know what twisting might come to them because of this particular pain.

Should we meet again, I will open another door of knowing for him as well. I will tell him that there are ways to shape oneself through loss that leave room for the heart and the soul to grow. Like a painter who realizes that his work cannot hold its original intent, we must learn to put down the brush and walk away from what has become unsustainable. This dad must begin the long, hard journey of walking away from the image of the family as it has been toward the family as it is. This is mandatory. He must admit that all has changed; that nothing looks as it should.

We must all do this at one time or another.

From there we must watch carefully and honestly for what is true for us in our own particular grief. One might crawl into bed from exhaustion, one might become numb, one might lash out and one might armor oneself against all such experiences and move back toward school or work as if nothing of import has happened at all. There are a thousand faces to grief and we must allow room for the witnessing of what is true for any, for ourselves, in each particular loss. Then and only then can we begin the artful process of losing — of looking directly at the brokenness within us, naming the damage done, and then bringing permission, and then forgiveness, and one day love to that damage.

A story is told about the Japanese shogun Ashikaga Yoshimasa who sent a damaged Chinese tea bowl back to China for repairs in the late 15th century. When it was returned, repaired with ugly metal staples, Yoshimasa prompted Japanese craftsmen to look for a more aesthetic means of repair. They began to join the shards of broken pottery with a lacquer laced with powdered gold, creating an object that displayed its flaws while becoming whole once more. The art form, *Kintsukuroi*, or golden repair, became so popular that a philosophy emanated from its artistry. Both the imperfections and the repairs were seen simply as events in the life of the object, allowing its life to continue in service to its purpose. Flaws and imperfections were embraced as an acceptance of the eventual brokenness of things and were understood to reflect the natural journey of life itself.

Sherri and Seth Mandell understand this. After the loss of their young son, Koby, they stepped back into life bit by bit, evidence of fractures everywhere, in their faces, their walk, their very breathing. Eventually they decided to form an organization to provide respite for families who had also lost someone due to war and they arranged a retreat for their first guests. They merged their pain with purpose, a lacing of gold. The Koby Mandell Foundation opened its doors in 2001. Families with similar losses gathered in Israel for healing and sharing, art and play. Parents hugged each other, told their stories, made meals together. Siblings learned that they weren't the only family touched by hate. Laughter bubbled now and then. At the end of the summer, after spending time with other children who had lost someone to terror, Sherri's daughter Eliana explained why she liked camp so much. "It's like we touched each other's hearts...we put our hearts together and we made a new heart."

This is the art of losing, *Kintsukuroi*.

When I next meet with the dad and his children I will see the tracelines of the wounds they will carry and my own breaklines will burn in recognition. I never wished this fragility for myself, never wanted to bear the scars of my brother's death; nor do I wish to see the same in them and yet, only because I know these lines, only because I too have suffered, can I possibly mirror for them how to live scarred.

I will give them permission to feel all that they feel, to be crazy in the ways that are natural for them. One client I had insisted that we never call her dead husband by name as that would invite his ghost near her and she needed to know that he had moved on in peace. So for weeks we only spoke of him as 'him' until the sharp edge of her grief began to shift and she could no longer not speak his name. I will give this dad and his children room to be crazy and wise about what they most need and I will speak to them of compassion ... how they will be cut over and over again because of this cruel losing, and how we can soften the fire of those cuts the tiniest bit by being kind to ourselves. No one does this impeccably I will say. No one knows how it really feels for any of us. Anything other than kindness makes this worse. The art of losing is about facing the truth, witnessing in what particular ways the sculpture of our being is breaking, and then bringing benevolence to that breaking. Pieces will fall to the floor, bits of our dreams, the strengths we thought defined us will lie scattered around, we won't be intact. For a time, we will know brokenness.

And I will show them what is possible. I'll hold alive the story of the Mandells and Madonna Badger and Viktor Frankl and of my friend Scotty, who rebuilt first his home and then his life. I'll remind them that they are not alone in their suffering. In brokenness there is value still and the mirroring of what is natural in our mortal world. With our scarred, rent bodies we may find purpose. We are vessels yet, able to carry the waters of the heart. The golden joining is available to us all.

PART TWO
HAPPINESS

AND

"We think the world apart," wrote Parker Palmer, perhaps the West's most astute educator of educators and in so doing we create separations where none need exist. We become caught by either/or, black-or-white thinking and fail to hold what Nobel Prize winning physicist, Neils Bohr, proposed: "The opposite of a fact is falsehood, but the opposite of a profound truth may very well be another profound truth." In the physics of recovery from loss we find happier-ness in this knowledge and do best when we let go of rigid thoughts or rigid patterns of emotion and behavior and step into the *and* of possibility. We can be shattered *and* heal. Hearts do break *and* grow in love and courage and capacity. Our pain may be excruciating *and* there is a way to live such that life shimmers with meaning and joy and we find ourselves laughing and dancing and celebrating even as we deeply miss what had been true. And, and, and.

I often do this exercise now with my students. At the beginning of a day-long retreat on happiness I'll draw a rough looking circle on a large piece of flip-chart paper and ask the audience to shout out words that define their current stressors. Phrases fly toward me at the speed of falcons: "overwhelm," "the to-do list," "my boss," "paperwork," "back pain," "my broken car," "aging body," "not enough money," "not enough time," "fear," "abandonment," "stuck-ness," "my marriage," "my divorce," "my kids," "death," "illness," losing my mind." In five minutes the circle is overfull and we christen the thing 'the swamp.' The swamp holds our pains, fears, worries, stressors (real and imagined), and disappointments. Simply labeling the swamp brings the energy in the room down and with each new word added I can see the students become sadder, heavier, weary.

I continue the class. We learn tools and principles of positivity, we discuss the freedom to choose and the possibility of the *and*. We begin to offer stories of those who have risen from tragic circumstances and highlight in our own lives when we too have grown, put ourselves back together with a bit of gold lacquer and duct tape. Laughter bubbles up. We'll exchange stories of the absurdity of life — the "you can't make this shit up" stuff — and they'll begin to top each other.

"My mother died, and then the dogs ate poison and croaked right on the back porch, and in the same night, the night of her funeral, I found out that my spouse had been cheating on me with my best friend."

"Really?" someone else will shout out. "That's nothing; let me tell you about my last three years."

And the game is on ... whose life has been hardest, who has seen the most?

The laughter continues, how could it not, this stuff cannot be invented and when the room has had its fill of the ludicrousness and cruelty of it all, I'll turn the swamp page of the flip chart over and on the very next page draw a rough outline of a circle. I'll ask them then to share with me what they are grateful for in their lives. New words emerge: "sunshine after a long winter," "my partner," "the fact that I'm still living," "friends," "acts of kindness," "meaningful work," "birthday parties," "music," "dancing," "the gate guy at work who smiles every morning." And old terms show up, this time from the perspective of appreciation: "my kids," "my marriage," "my boss," "my body." The terms overspill. There is not enough room for all we appreciate.

I then flick the "swamp" circle page back on top of our gratitude circle and begin to move it up and down, like a cartoon flip book. As I do so the students quiet. What is true becomes obvious. It's the same life. The swamp, the pond of gratitude ... it's the same life, same days, same elements. Our stressors and our happiness co-exist.

What matters is the *and* here ... we can focus on what makes life hard and miserable and stop there or we can acknowledge what makes life hard and miserable, work with it, make healthy choices about the swamp *and* see the good as well. Tal Ben-Shahar, world thought-leader in the field of positive psychology, teaches us about the *and* when considering growth and healing during dark times in his books *Happier* and *Being Happy* because it enables us to live into paradox. We can be in pain, experience despair, make mistakes, be filled with anxiety or fear *and* choose practices and perspectives that sustain us.

This wisdom is seen as well in the work done by Jim Collins and Jerry Porras in their exploration of great organizations and their leadership. In their work, *Built To Last*, they refer to this as the "genius of the and," explaining that truly visionary companies are led by those who embrace both ends of continuums: continuity *and* change, predictability *and* chaos, heritage *and* renewal.

Two profound truths do appear then to co-exist when considering how to live life well despite its ups and downs: Suffering does not negate what is good and rich in our world; what is good and rich in our world exists bounded by our suffering. Both are real. Both are valid. Both deserve attention. To rise after loss, to find that which brings about a life worth living even with its despairs is to attend to both and keep our minds open to the possibility of *And*.

"The same world, to different minds,
is a heaven, and a hell."

~ Ralph Waldo Emerson

Heaven Within Hell

A uthor and speaker Mark Matusek is a virile
man. To stand next to him is to stand next to
a body that radiates power, energy, consciousness.
Everything about him demonstrates an undeniable
masculinity — his broad sculpted chest, his strong
firm grip, his stance, which is often like that of a
guardian — legs slightly apart, hips even, head up
and searching. His questions to his audiences as he
teaches about the transformations within dark times
are fierce, probing, provocative. He casts a warrior's
glance ... searching for the truth under the stories
we all tell ourselves. But within his eyes, another
energy emerges. To be caught in his gaze is to be
caught in the gaze of the Quan Yin, the Goddess of
mercy and compassion in the Mahayana Buddhist
tradition; she is known for her unbreachable love
for humanity. Mark balances the paradox of the
feminine within the masculine with ease and grace,

he is embodied Kintsukuroi. This balance seems possible because of his direct experience of hell and his ability to find heaven exactly there.

Many of his stories will suffice to support this embodiment but I offer only one here, from his early life. When he was nineteen, his older sister, the woman who had been his constant caretaker, came to him in despair. Her marriage broken, her heart unmoored, she found herself in an unconquerable depression. She arrived for tea one evening, a shell of her former vibrant self and asked her younger brother a question. "How do you live?" At nineteen, on the cusp of adulthood, the question was bigger than Mark could grasp, and he floundered, offering platitudes and mumblings that all would be well. He truly could not yet offer her anything sustaining; to answer such a question definitively takes nearly a lifetime.

She left the next morning; this visit would be her last as three weeks later she took her own life. Her question, the one he could not answer, became a bell call for Mark. He began a long odyssey to find an answer that would suffice.

How do we live when all is dark?

By finding and holding onto the heaven within hell.

There is a richness that is available to us directly in our suffering; a deep learning that can occur when all that is superficial is stripped away and we are at the essence of things. Mark, quoting Roethke, says this, "'In a dark time, the eye begins to see.' With our illusions of safety exploded, outside the bounds of 'normal' life ... new abilities do indeed dawn in a person; values, intuitions, skills, perspectives that might seem unnatural to those who've led more sheltered lives."

Helen Keller, blind and deaf from birth, offers us a direct clarity: "We could never learn to be brave and patient, if there were only joy in the world." And "Character cannot be developed in ease and quiet. Only through experience of trial and suffering can the soul be strengthened, vision cleared, ambition inspired, and success achieved."

Viktor Frankl, too, reminds us of the heaven possible — the vision cleared — within our own minds, our capacity to shift our attention away from destruction, toward imaginations that sustain us. In the bitter ground of Auschwitz, in his mind, he wrote the text for his theory of how we survive well the tragedies of our lives. Dreaming the lectures he would give to his students, he lived the very model of resilience and will toward meaning that he would later teach.

And I know this: In the time of my brother's dying I knew heaven. In the instant of that morning, sunlit and springlike, one by one we stood near him, leaned over, and spoke impossible words. "I love you John. It's okay. You can go." Right now writing this, I don't know how we, those who loved him longest and deepest, did that. To reconstruct the bravery required to do such a thing feels, from a distance, gargantuan. But I do know this ... in that moment, when called to offer someone you love the freedom to leave a body bounded by pain, you experience heaven. Love emerges bottomless without border or agenda. The heart can literally become so big and so clear and so radiant, so burnished, that it sends you forward, and the mouth opens and a grace rises through you that in no other moment would you ever be able to manifest. "You are free to go. We love you. We will never stop loving you."

Years after his sister's suicide, after decades of speaking with many people marked by intense suffering, Mark offers this: " ...you conjure your future from white space, locate the hidden person, yourself, against this unfamiliar background, peering through grief and loss at something greater ...I knew (a) strange exultation myself, of being destroyed yet beyond destruction ...a retrieved sense of sacredness, even transcendence, flooding the vacuum of survival where common protections had been stripped away. Terror does have its purposes."

There is a kind of heaven within hell. There lies wisdom accessible no other way.

Heaven Within Hell Part 2

Happiness after loss looks like a bone-bare tree in winter. Empty of growth, steady yet silent. We are compelled by the bareness of the thing, the rawness, and each branch points seemingly randomly, meaninglessly . . . as if any one of the limbs taken or climbed would bring us to the exact same place — an endpoint facing relentless sky.

At the beginning of our journey happiness is hidden. Yet it is so important to suspect that as potential it remains present. We may be saying and thinking, "I will never recover from this," yet still we find ourselves breathing, still we find ourselves huddled by fire as if to warm our own cold limbs, still, yet, we seek the tiniest signs of life — a hummingbird — a butterfly — a rising star. We're drawn to notice a promise of what yet might be. A woman who lost her youngest daughter at the age of 6, a girl born with a seizure disorder so fierce the doctors suspected she would not live to see one year said to me, "I know this will be bad for a really long time, until it's a little less bad, and then a little less bad. Until I know that I am in a better place I have to believe that that is how it will go."

Just as we cannot ask the dogwood to live in full bloom at all times, nor ignore its cyclical nature of life, death, life, so too we cannot ask of ourselves happiness immediately after loss. That would be aberration. We can sense, or hope for, the experience of pain lightening little by little. We can ask this: "Let me notice that which is good in the world to sustain me." This is the other form of heaven within hell . . . the capacity to see the good in the world and hold onto it.

When Australian Olympic skiing athlete, Janine Shepard, found herself paralyzed, strapped to a bed in a hospital spinal injury ward that would be her home for months, she recalled a moment unlike any other. She had been struck by a speeding truck on her last pre-Olympic training ride. The accident caused her spine to fragment. Lying tied to the bed, not knowing if she would ever walk again, depression ensued. She began to give up and marveled that others in the room — paraplegics and quadriplegics — had found a will to survive. She could only address the four others in the room by speaking and they could barely see each other through mirrors positioned above their beds. She felt horribly alone. One night a nurse brought straws. She had each of them hold on to a straw while she carefully linked each straw to another and then another until the straws traversed the five beds in a circle of connection. "There," she said. "Now we are all linked together." That physical connection became a true lifeline for Janine; she chose to live.

Savoring this moment of joining through the months of physical therapy and adjustment to a full body cast, and then braces, and then eventually crutches, is an example of Janine holding onto that which is good. It is so easy sometimes, especially when we are in pain, to see only the pain, only the suffering, to notice as Rilke reminds us the stone that is in our face. And yet, the resilient among us, the happiest among us, find a way to see that which is beneficent or light-filled or joyous. This is a natural impulse, hardwired and universal that we only need remember to nurture. Witnessing my nieces' and nephews' friends climb the stairs to comfort each other the day of my brother's death was a gift; remembering it, appreciating it for what it meant about our capacity to be humane, was an act of hope, a deliberate choice to find heaven in hell. Here is where a seed of happiness begins to germinate, in the awareness of that which sustains us.

And as we learn to savor the good, we find that we begin to see the world through the lens of positivity.

We notice that no matter how dark the day, light exists. We remember that our strains, our losses, our fears are real, and virtue is also real. Generosity abounds. Kindness exists on street corners and in restaurant bathrooms and train station waiting rooms. We take in evidence of smiles, caresses and laughter, and in a gentle, unseen manner, we begin aligning our brain toward becoming happier. Not in such a way that we deny the hell that surrounds us...but in such a way that we begin to infuse that hell with what is also always real: the good in this life; the good within us.

What Happiness
Looks Like

According to Tal Ben-Shahar, happiness is a balance of both meaning and pleasure. To be happy in this world we need a bit of both; the balance will be unique for each, shifting according to our age, development and circumstance. What brought meaning and uplift at age 23 will be different than what brings delight at 46. During times of ease, few of us have difficulty naming what would make us happier. But what about the moments following betrayal...when a father returns home to discover his wife's suicide? Or the long, slow return from the depths of a depression so deep we cannot remember if we ever knew how to laugh? What is happiness then? Where is pleasure...a seemingly ridiculous word...when so much is life-rending?

Clues exist, seeds left by those who have survived well when life dealt its worst card.

Anne Lamott (after the death of her best friend): "And I felt like my heart had been so thoroughly and irreparably broken that there could be no real joy again, that at best there might eventually be a little contentment. Everyone wanted me to get help and rejoin life, pick up the pieces and move on, and I tried to, I wanted to, but I just had to lie in the mud with my arms wrapped around myself, eyes closed, grieving, until I didn't have to anymore."

The quiet seed of return shows first through her arms wrapped around herself in compassion, laced with a patience to wait out the anvil-like press of grief.

Viktor Frankl: "We who lived in concentration camps can remember the men who walked through the huts comforting others, giving away their last piece of bread. They may have been few in number, but they offer sufficient proof that everything can be taken from a man but one thing: the last of the human freedoms — to choose one's attitude in any given set of circumstances, to choose one's own way."

The choice to choose who one is in response...uplift appears here.

Ranier Maria Rilke: "Everything is in my face and everything in my face is stone. Break in; and let your great transforming happen to me and my great grief cry happen to you."

Rilke reaching forward to another, in this case the divine, begging to trade experience — let your great transforming energy happen to me and take my grief cry, he pleads. Here we see the move toward connection, the evidence of motion in reaching for another.

Pema Chodron: "Instead of asking ourselves, 'How can I find security and happiness?' we could ask ourselves, 'Can I touch the center of my pain? Can I sit with suffering, both yours and mine, without trying to make it go away? Can I stay present to the ache of loss or disgrace — disappointment in all its many forms — and let it open me?'"

The tender heart opening to what is, remaining present to ache in its unique form, a careful, mindful attention to the nightmare as it is, a seed exists here too.

The return toward happiness is not a fixed path. Each assault brings its own potential solution. After my brother died I sought evidence from the universe of spirits and called on psychics and mediums. Was it possible, I needed to know, to find a way to feel his hand in mine, as I had so often when we were both little and the world still had promise? The possibility of crossing barriers of space and time engaged me and offered a bridge toward hope. This felt meaningful to me. Pleasure took much longer to reappear.

During the time of my divorce, a heartbreak of years, music returned me to myself . . . dancing in the early morning hours while my children slept so that I could feel life in my body. The touch of joy existed here.

And when a dear friendship failed, and I lost not only that friend, but also the companionship of many, happiness began to show itself through conscious small gestures of self-love. I began to engage in a daily practice of early morning remembering of what I valued about myself and this built a courage within me to reach out to others bit by bit.

Just as each physical wound asks of the body a diversity of related healing responses; each insult to the heart requires a particular composition of choices. What the return will look like for you cannot be foretold by what it has looked like for another. There is no one way; there is only the way that nourishes you.

*"There is life without love. It is not worth a bent penny,
or a scuffed shoe."*

~ Mary Oliver

Love

A woman, Margaret, approached me after class once to ask a private question. Her fiancé, at the age of 49, had been diagnosed with Lou Gehrig's disease (ALS). They were a second love for each other, and all had been beautiful, according to Margaret, until the disease appeared five months prior. The wedding had been planned, the rings purchased, the flowers ordered. Guests would arrive in a month's time and she would wear a dress of blue-grey, the color of the ocean she said, near their Maine home. After their wedding they would leave for two weeks in Spain. Everything they had always wanted had seemed to be unfolding. She had been afraid to even voice her question in her hometown for fear it would somehow get back to Peter, her beloved. But here, in a different state, attending a one-day retreat on happiness, she wanted to risk the question. I sat down near her and nodded for her to begin.

"I wonder," she said. "Am I doing the right thing?"

ALS is a relentless journey of losing ground, she continued. She was absolutely right...there is little respite to the physical symptoms, which can be myriad, in addition to the frequent appearance of profound depression and/or anxiety. I remained silent. This was not a question with a simple answer.

"When are you happiest?" I asked.

"When I am with him," Margaret answered.

"Even on the dark days?" I countered.

She nodded, yes, even on the dark days.

"I can't answer this question for you," I replied, fear taking over. I did not want responsibility for her life choice.

"But you can," she said.

I raised my brow.

"You know what people say when they are ready to die. That's what I want to know. Will I regret this when I am dying...if I should leave him now because I am afraid of the progression, will I regret this?"

I thought of a hundred therapeutic responses in

the space of a breath which would let me off the
hook so that she could find her way into her own
answer. Who really could possibly ever answer this
question for another? Pat responses came to mind:
"Each person must choose for themselves." Or
"That's not how it works with a therapist; we would
need time to explore this."

I opened my mouth to offer a kind but neutral
statement and out of my mouth came this: "No one
dies regretting having invested in love."

I didn't know that I knew that until I spoke it.

Sometimes words have the impact of swords. As
they flew toward Margaret, I knew them to be true.
We regret overworking. We regret fighting. We
regret not doing the things we had always promised
ourselves we would do or see what we most wanted
to see. But no one in my experience of sitting with
others on the threshold of death had ever lamented
moving toward love.

"There is life without love," writes Mary Oliver.
"It is not worth a bent penny, or a scuffed shoe."
When it calls you, she commands, "when you hear,
a mile away and still out of sight, the churn of the
water as it begins to swirl and roil ... when you hear
that unmistakable pounding ... and sense ahead the
embattlement, the long falls plunging and steaming
— then row, row for your life toward it."

The heart of happiness during the darkest times — after the murder of a child, the racing arc of a bomb, the disintegration of a marriage — appears here, in the waters of love. A life without love during times of ease is devoid of color, of wind and warmth. A life without love when tragedy strikes or pain swells is excruciating — a tearing of one apart.

Connection to others is crucial to a life of well-being. This is found to be true in the tribal peoples of the east and the city-dwellers of the west and all other groups around the globe. We do well when we are in relationship to others; any path toward happiness after loss is made possible by the surround of love.

Did my answer help Margaret? I do not know.

Was it proper to offer such a strong declaration? Perhaps yes, perhaps no.

Am I glad those words flew from my mouth? Yes. For no other reason than this: such a clear declaration offered her a steady position from which to leap toward or something firm to push against ... her own reaction to my statement is what will most help her know what is true for her. And, this as well: sometimes we don't know what we believe until language flies directly out of us. Now I know, now I remember. Despite the accumulation of losses in my life and the unpredictability of love, here is where I long to go ... toward those rushing falls, that plunge.

*"Drink your tea slowly and reverently ...
Only this moment is life."*

~ *Thich Nhat Han*

The Surround of Love:
Loving Ourselves First

Only this moment is life. Only in this present moment do we have the power to choose how to move forward in our journey of recovery from loss. To drink our tea slowly, to sit in the stillness that implies is an act of mindfulness ... of holding time still so that we may be present. And in this gift to ourselves ... of steady still holding ... of savoring tea ... of quieting time ... we love ourselves. The surround of love that nourishes healing and opens a return to happiness is not only about love from others, it also contains the radical act of affection toward ourselves. We often believe that healing requires something coming toward us from the larger world — the care of others, wisdom from the divine or a masterful guide, a chance meeting with a stranger who knows exactly what we are feeling.

These absolutely help and yet they will not hold if they are not bounded to a belief within ourselves, however small, that we matter and that we deserve to love ourselves through into a new living.

For some, turning our focus toward ourselves first, before others, is an unusual act, an extreme one. For others, self-regard is a daily practice. It does not matter which end of the spectrum you were on before ... before darkness arose. What does matter is your capacity to remember that every act of self-love is an act of care, of hope, and of honor. We honor our very life force when we attend to ourselves in a kind way.

Drink your tea slowly and reverently, as if it matters. As if the nourishment of your body in such a simple, direct way matters ... and it does. All other wisdom about gathering happiness after loss rests on our ability to bring toward ourselves that which sustains us. Before we can thread together a life that rises in the presence of sorrow we must include loving ourselves through acts of care. When we do so, we can begin to experience the world as if love and hope and goodness do exist. When we fail to do so, we see and know only pain. It is that simple.

The first step when tragedy strikes is to breathe, to remain alive; a first step on our return toward a life with happiness is self-regard, to keep alive within us the flame of care by loving our own tender, broken beings. That might look like tea. It might look like returning to our beds, each night, with the exact right blankets under which to nestle. It sometimes looks like giving ourselves permission to lean on others for help, a call out in the dark, 3am, "Please come, I'm not sure how to make it through this night." And it may appear in small gestures of self-care: a lit candle, or a song, or a settling in front of a window, watching the land be itself without care or cause, its stillness a balm, its surety a gift.

Connection to others matters greatly . . . and yet without loving connection toward our own self those outer connections don't hold; they are never quite enough. Even if we have had a life in which we are accustomed to self-criticism or self-loathing, any day can still become the day in which we choose to say, "I wish to love myself a little bit more today," an affirmation that becomes the foundation for all acts of self care. Because we have only one life in this form, and because no one else can live our unique life, and because life will bring us a particular array of sufferings with which to cope, we must find the way to self regard. No one else can provide this for us . . . and we are the perfect source for our own eventual return to a happier life through loving ourselves first.

I would never wish for others the strains I have had to manage and the sorrows I have had to endure, and yet each passage of difficulty has brought with it the opportunity to love again the "stranger who was myself," to quote the poet Derek Walcott, and to find a way to nourish myself with an awakening awareness that I matter and I am worthy.

Grounded Optimism

One of the statements I hear frequently after someone has lost a child is the following: "I don't know what to hope for anymore." It's as if the blow has not only damaged the present but thrown into question the possibility of any sort of future that holds a sense of the good. And there is a deep truth to this not knowing . . . we cannot imagine in the midst of loss what could grow, what new might emerge. Yet, as we travel the wheel of life long enough, we begin to notice a parallel truth: life continues on in its own way and things change. The searing pain of the first few months shifts to a dull constant ache that shifts to a surprising moment of laughter on a day, and then back once more to ache, and then one day we simply notice that the pain is not what it was and we have entered into the world with our eyes a bit more open and our hearts slightly more intact.

And if we hold to our definition of true hope, facing reality as it is and at the same time opening the door to a slightly better future, then we have an idea about how to move forward with a bit of optimism. The optimism I'm suggesting we consider here is not a Disney-style-bluebird-of-happiness-unicorns-dancing-in-the-meadow kind of optimism. It is what Tal Ben-Shahar calls "grounded optimism," positivity that does not negate or ignore reality but rather embraces it and considers whatever is in front of us to enjoy, savor, or celebrate. It is Janine Shepard celebrating the day that she moved from a full body cast to leg braces. Although reality dictated that she would never again be an Olympic skier, still that shift from one level of disability to a different one was worth acknowledging. It opened the door to a slightly better future and in the present it afforded her the grace of recognition that life had moved on. She was no longer who she had been on the Olympic team but she was also no longer who she was the day of the accident when many thought her life was over.

Optimism is a cornerstone of both resilience and happiness. Those who live thriving lives even in the presence of great distress tend to be optimistic: cheerful, buoyant, enthusiastic. Once someone has begun to realize that they don't know what to hope for, the very question itself implies an inkling of awareness that things might be better; we just don't know how or in what shape. So, to bolster positivity, to begin to move toward a life with a slightly better future, we might practice mindfulness, which over time boosts positivity. We might surround ourselves with others who have suffered and found their way back into joy. We could notice our pessimistic thoughts and each time we notice ask ourselves, "Is there any other story or belief that I might hold?" We might invite ourselves to move — exercise is the most efficient, universal anti-depressant available because of its impact on our neurochemistry. It physically changes the brain we find ourselves in ... which then changes our emotional state ... which then creates a sense of a bit more heaven in hell. All of these are options, and here is one more that I love, one that I practiced during the months after my brother died, my marriage fell apart and my financial situation became rocky and unpredictable.

Every night, right before closing my eyes, I would ask myself, "What was the great moment today?" I didn't write it down or process the answer. I simply asked the question and then scanned the day for the great moment. What I began to notice, over time, was the following: Every day had a great moment. Sometimes they were small ... the appearance of a hummingbird at my feeder. Sometimes they were wondrous ... a baby born, an unexpected reunion, a message from my daughter thanking me, "*Mom, there is so much you have done for me and so many ways you continue to inspire me. You have taught me to value my happiness. You have taught me about self care and*

*how it is important to do what you love ... You are an
artist of your own life – each stroke carries you farther in
your path. Thank you."*

I began to notice something else: because I knew I
would ask this question of myself at night, I began
to be in the day looking for the good, for that great
moment, and so my vision shifted. Even while in
pain and with relentless anxiety about the future, my
heart and brain were in concert, scanning the day
for the good. The question, too, became a part of my
lexicon. I'd be walking with a friend, see the stroke
of a hawk arcing toward the land, and find myself
saying, "There, that's the great moment today." My
friend would ask about my words and I'd share the
practice and we'd begin to text each other our great
moments, now and then, and in this way my expe-
rience of the good became communal and broader.

Any new habit, such as going to bed with a positive
question in mind, creates new neuronal pathways. I
knew that eventually, if I persevered, I would create
a new mindset for myself...one that could hold the
good in the day even as I rode the waves of grief.
But this knowing, that experience of a new brain,
felt far less important initially than the experience
of being in the day in a different way. I brought this
tool to a teen once, a high school senior, with lym-
phoma. As she finished treatment we talked about
how she wanted to shape the future of the weeks
ahead. Without hair, having lost a boyfriend and

some friends through the course of her illness, she felt as though she were starting anew. I offered her this practice ... the best moment of the day ... as a way to fill the spaciousness that frightened her. In my final call with her, after she had been home two weeks, she told me of the tiny moments of uplift that had sustained her. A visit from her aunt. The aroma of her mother's coffee in the morning. A surprise discovery one day — a word etched in a sidewalk brick: "Love."

We cannot change what is. Hope may seem a far distance away. But we can change how we see our day. We can attend to what is good, each day, for a moment here and a moment there, and in this way begin to build an optimism that is real and sustaining, allowing for reality as it is — with both its sharpness and its graces.

Courage

June 6, 2009. A dear friend's husband gone in a flash — plane crash. My friend left with two small children; normal gone in the space of four seconds, the length of time it took for the plane to shatter against a lake. Same day, a colleague drove herself to the Triboro Bridge, a three-hour drive. Parked her small grey Honda on the bridge. Got out of the car. Took off her shoes. Climbed the scaffolding, held on and then, not. One day. Two deaths. I found myself on the tile of my floor after the news of the second loss skyrocketed in, keening, hearing only the sounds of Rilke's voice in my head ... "Everything in my face is stone. I can see no way out and no way through." Minutes became hours before I could move again. The next day I couldn't function. I poured boiling hot water on my hand instead of into my cup and gave up for a day. Bed was the only place I could imagine being, staring at the surprising sky, my mind locked in disbelief.

Sometimes it is impossible to remember beauty in this world, or kindness. To remember and to find our way through, back out of stone, requires courage.

We must be brave to seek happiness once stricken, for we only do so with a profound awareness that horrible things might occur again at any moment. Many of us grew up with superstitions about bad things happening in threes, or the power of a particular moon cycle to bring about evil. These are primitively embedded beliefs that seek to protect us though we all understand at some level how feeble they are and how capricious life is. Once struck it is nigh impossible to pretend that all will always be well. I know now, at a cellular level, that one terrible bit of news can easily be followed by a second within seconds. To journey toward a smile in the face of such awareness is optimistic at best, and courageous at its core.

To be brave means to take a risk in the face of obstacles . . . and in terms of happiness the greatest obstacles live within. To choose a happier life, one of pleasure and meaning and openness to wonder means to hold clearly the awareness of life's upheavals and bald nastiness while seeking the nourishment of what is rich or shimmery, soothing or inspiring, heart-opening and soul-soaring. To some this may not seem like such an astonishing act but to many of us, the movement toward happiness means the letting go of family structures and beliefs that served to keep us locked in to pessimism, even despair. So often my students have said to me, "It's alright that my marriage failed, I never really thought I'd have a happy life anyway." Or, "Of course my husband would lose his job, everything bad that could happen, happens to me." Or, "Life sucks and there is nothing I can do about it." Every time we hear ourselves say this, but still choose a practice that lifts us, we embrace the courage of leaving behind history to seek a new destiny.

"We develop courage by couraging," wrote Mary Daly. When the voices without seek to keep us small, or our own inner dialogue argues with us to remain disbelieving of life's bounty, here is what helps to move forward with valor: Dance anyway. Seek laughter regularly. Mindfully ask ourselves, what would make me 3 percent happier in this moment? Who could I call? What could I do? What can I read or listen to or build? What might I say to myself if I chose not to believe that I was doomed to misery and life was hell? If I were a person who loved life ... what would I think, right now, in this very moment? And if I were a joyful person, exactly how much zest would I bring to the next conversation, the next meal, my next step outside into this world?

We learn courage by couraging and we nourish happiness by these brave acts of uplift. And this isn't about simply getting on, pulling oneself out of bed and up by one's bootstraps as our grandfathers used to advise. Sustaining courage involves passion and tenacity. The dogged pursuit of the choice to be vital and vivacious, to bring our whole hearts to life. The word courage came "from the Latin word cor, meaning heart, and the original definition was to tell the story of who you are with your whole heart," writes Brene Brown. To do so requires us to bring back with us into the day the lines of shattering...and through these lines begin to perceive, and then act from, the light that burns within.

Courage, we find, is contagious. As we move with bravery toward shaping a day that lifts us, or strengthens us, we find we want to exercise yet more bravery. My choice to practice tunnel climbing and rope climbing, courage in the physical realm, spurred the courage to engage in online dating after a two-year hiatus. And that ridiculously brave act engendered a deeper act of bravery, one in which I reshaped my work life in order to create space, not only for a new love, but for new joy in my life. Courage begets courage and the contagion effect is evident within us and around us. With each move toward a braver life, we model for others the ability to be brave even when scarred, shattered, and on somewhat shaky ground.

There is no perfect time for bravery. That moment is always now.

A student of mine, diagnosed with stage four breast cancer, her third diagnosis in ten years, spends her days offering free hugs to veterans on the streets of Syracuse. Each time she does so, she brings her heart to theirs, holds for a moment, and then lets go. With each hug, her heart synchronizes to theirs and their hearts become, albeit briefly, connected. She is a model for us and a guide. In the labyrinth of illness, she has chosen to love. Her story now includes arms that hold many, a practice that invites the whole world in, and a heart unrelentingly kind.

*"Everyone deserves at least one person who
thinks they are the bread of heaven."*

~Clarissa Pinkola Estes

The Choir

I learned of my brother's illness on a Wednesday
afternoon. That night I packed and the next
morning flew to his home in North Carolina. That
evening while jamming shirts into my suitcase, in
shock and rising panic, I wrote an email to my four
closest friends. Sharing John's news, and my expec-
tations of an abbreviated life for him, I asked them
two things: first to be with me as I needed them
every moment of the journey, and second, to help
me find my way back into the world after this time
had passed. Four years have come and gone since
I buried my brother and these friends continue to
remain present. Their love is constant and deep
and reminds me, when I can remember, that I am
not alone.

In every trespass through darkness, companionship
is the rope we seek, the cable that enables to us to

climb, first into the cave, and then out once more. As we emerge, we discover that some of our friends are still there, holding sustenance, bread and water at the entrance, and some have faded. We learn as well that new companions have found their way next to us, which may or may not be a good thing, and some old companions, toxic ones, persist. One day it will be time to choose. The land at the exit of the cave is new, uncertain, and our fellowship has been altered. Who we will invest in, where we will put our energy, and which bonds we will sever? These are the questions that begin to arise.

Goethe wrote this, "Tell a wise person or else keep silent." In terms of a life with uplift in it, I suggest this, "Invest in the choir only; everyone else, let fade." The choir is made up of those who believe we are the bread of heaven. Those we deeply trust and who trust us. The companions who are willing to hold back the webs and moss that line the entrance of the cave so that we may go through, and who light the path with their care and kindness. They send you ridiculously funny cards at the height of your despair and fly hundreds of miles to be with you the day you take your niece shopping for a dress to wear at her father's funeral. They offer you, in other words, their whole hearts. Everyone else we can let fade as the edges of our pain begin to soften. We have grown through our travail into new beings and only those who serve to appreciate our growth belong near us.

"This world was made to be free in," David Whyte teaches. "Give up all other worlds except the one to which you belong ... Anything or anyone that does not bring you alive is too small for you." This does not mean we need to fully divorce ourselves from anyone who does not honor who we have become. It does mean we need to divorce ourselves from the habit of spending too much time and energy on them and instead marry ourselves more deeply to those who lift us. We, who have been through the cave, know that we don't have time to waste time on friendships that no longer serve.

Consider this: each time we move away from poisonous commitments, we clear a path within our heart for someone new to arrive who regards us well. We open space in the world to be surprised ...by the type of hello that warms us fully and the kind of glance that reminds us that we are, in fact, significant.

One day this will become clear:

Choose your choir.

Love who you love and who love you.

Clear out the rest.

There is no time to waste on bonds that make life heavier.

Holding on and Letting Go

August, 1992. My first day of training as a psychologist at the Dana-Farber Cancer Institute in Boston where I would be working with children diagnosed with cancer. Within five minutes of walking through the door I received the chart for my first patient, a boy, aged five, with a recurrence of lymphoma. His parents chose to return to the Farber for bone marrow transplant and within the space of that morning I would meet them, him, I'll call him Matt, and settle him into the ward over at our neighboring children's hospital. He would sail through bone marrow, live another seven years, and die as his 12th year began. When I received news of his death, I thought about the theme that had been resonant with me that year at the Farber, one offered me by my hypnotherapy professor. "Life," he used to say, "is about holding on and letting go, and knowing when to do each."

As they buried their son, Matt's parents, Paul and Julie, began the long slow journey of letting go…and of learning what they could now hold onto with a sense of surety. Months after his loss, they would write to me, and tell me how they had found a way to do so by praying to him every day…telling him about their day, asking for his wisdom from the etheric realms, and letting him know that their love rushed toward him still, a torrent, a channel, a river.

Holding on and letting go; happiness is about this as well. Knowing what we need to bring forth in order to experience uplift and knowing what to quell, what to soften and what to say goodbye to, that's our task. One action cannot exist without the other, meaning that as we choose to bring something new toward us that will amplify joy, we have less energy to invest in those practices or people that no longer nourish us, so we naturally begin to let go. As I practice my early morning dancing, I am letting go of the pattern of depression that accompanied me through all my early years of waking. When I invite my natural buoyancy into my conversations, I let go of an entrenched fantasy that I had to be serious to be taken seriously, and that intensity was my only great strength. Turns out one can be fierce and fun, serious and playful…where was that lesson in middle school?

Letting go in the territory of suffering also requires a willingness as well to feel a little less victimized by life and a little more grounded in a sense of agency. Helen Keller, a soul of efficacy despite her travails, teaches: "Your success and happiness lies in you. Resolve to keep happy, and your joy and you shall form an invincible host against difficulties." Anne Frank, locked in that damned attic, a teenager for God's sake, knew this as well: "And finally I twist my heart round again, so that the bad is on the outside and the good is on the inside, and keep on trying to find a way of becoming what I would so like to be . . . " This twisting of the heart, letting go of a sense of martyrdom or victimhood and choosing to determine who one is in life is a keystone to greater happiness. To find current evidence of such wisdom we only need look to our Nobel Prize winner, Malala Yousafzai, who, having been attacked by terrorists, affirmed: "The terrorists thought they would change my aims and stop my ambitions, but nothing changed in my life except this: weakness, fear and hopelessness died. Strength, power and courage were born."

Each habit, or way of seeing, has its time and place and not all serve in all circumstances. During crossroad moments in our lives, it behooves us to consider that this might be the moment to practice a new way of being...to let go of, oh say, something that brings us pain and bring toward our living something that will lead to health or enlivenment or a sense of being more at home within our own bodies. In one of my workshops on resilience, I encountered a student in his sixties, in a multi-year-long recovery from an autoimmune disorder that compromised his health, his ability to work, and called into question every relationship close to him. In class he decided to let go of one belief: that vulnerability made him weak. When I invited him to share how he might go about this, he said that he had no idea since even considering shedding the belief about vulnerability made him feel vulnerable. All he wanted to do in that very moment, he said, was to shut down and stop talking.

I asked him to stay with me in the question for one more moment. He agreed, looking frankly terrified. I asked what it might be like to allow himself to be vulnerable for one minute a day, as an experiment. He looked like he would throw up right there on the oriental carpet in the retreat center den where we met. "All right then, so that was not helpful," I laughed. "What about reading about vulnerability a few minutes each day ... to get used to the territory by learning about other people's journeys?"

He nodded the tiniest nod.

"Okay."

"Okay," I returned.

I promised to suggest great reading material and we contracted to stay in touch. And here's what I know that he does not yet know. Choosing to let go of a rigid belief around vulnerability will strain him for a time; he will feel exposed, naked, at risk of losing himself. Then one day he will find himself in a moment in which every bone in his body will want to flee, a moment in an attic for example, when terror and despair will sit right next to broken frames and molded books, and instead of fleeing or raging he will find himself softening, opening his heart, knowing that even as the world was shit, he still so wants his life and this world and he can no longer lock himself into only desolation, he was no longer that guy, and he will know also that, in his bones, right next to the urge to flee or rage, right there deep in the marrow, lives also the urge to live and love again.

"Each creature speaks and spells one thing and the same,
'Myself,' it speaks and spells,
'what I do is me, for that I came.'"
~ Gerard Manley Hopkins

Becoming True

We have but one chance in this form to live the one life only we can create. There is no other person who can bring forward what is true and rich within us. We can choose to be in life as if it is our life to shape, a work of our own art, and in this way bring our fullness alive, or we can choose to become a mimic of someone else's choices, thus withholding from the world the specific and particular richness that only we can bring to bear.

This choice is deeply potent in a time of recovery as well as in times of ease. One of the realities of return to the world after loss is that there is no one path: because of this we are free to craft our return so that it serves us. Among the great misunderstandings that can make that process even harder is the belief that others are better at it, or that there is a specific formula we ought follow, or by becoming the recipient of life's arrow shots, we are somehow, at our core, wrong and therefore our choices in how we handle grief or anger or regret are also inherently wrong. As my friend Alex says, there is nothing we can't make worse through our own critical self-judgment.

What is true, what is ours, in crafting a life as we journey through shadow is just that: what is true for us. We must do our best to discern what is authentic as we journey toward our new normal. There is no healthier posture.

At its core, to be authentic means to be self-authoring, to shape each day as if we were the author of that day and the only story that needed to be written was our own. A few years after the murder of her eldest daughter, a friend of mine founded a Happiness Club in her local town. In another town, about 150 miles north, a friend whose middle son was killed in a car accident in his 17th year, devoted her life to raising money to combat drunk driving by becoming a yoga teacher. A portion of the proceeds from each class goes to support an annual fundraiser in her region against drunk driving. A third friend, bereft of her youngest child, makes a small yearly donation to a garden in her son's name. What is true for one may not be true for another and a gift exists for each of us in discovering who we are, uniquely, as we find our way back in to life.

That is the first layer of wisdom here.

A second layer: the more deeply we allow ourselves to be organically and fully shaped by experience, becoming the person who has seen and known this sort of uplift or that kind of sorrow, the more we are able to become the person we can and must be, given life's capricious sculpting. The poet Rilke, in a letter to his wife Clara, describes this insight after having apprenticed himself to the sculptor Rodin for an extended period of time.

"After all, works of art are always the result of one's having been in danger, of having gone through an experience all the way to the end, to where no one can go any further. The further one goes, the more private, the more personal, the more singular an experience becomes and the thing one is making is, finally, the necessary, irrepressible, and, as nearly as possible, definitive utterance of this singularity."

To consider our life as a work of art, one that is particular, is to invite in this possibility: that as we journey toward a new normal we are being shaped both by the forces that have pressed their weight upon us as well as by our singular understanding of those forces. If we allow ourselves freedom from other's expectations of how we ought be doing, or what we ought be doing, we move toward a natural expression of who we can be. As this occurs, we find that intersection that Hopkins pointed us toward, the place where who we are becomes what we do and what we do is inseparable from who we are. Here is where authenticity becomes manifest. Here is where we realize that life is neither something to be afraid of nor controlled, but an element as integral to the sculpting of ourselves as marble is to a statue or paint to a watercolor.

Here, at this juncture, the content of our life and the essence of our being blend and we become true.

"With an undefended heart, we can fall in love with life over and over every day."

~ *Tara Brach*

Undefended Hearts

A few years ago I found myself at the intersection of North, South, East and West Streets in my town. This joining, known as Park Circle, is where our business section flourishes. I was headed from West Street to North, looking for a place for coffee and a clear table upon which to write. On North Street, waiting to cross over to the other side, a woman in her mid-40s stood with a baby pack on her chest. From the distance of the one road between us, I couldn't see the baby, but I could see that the infant, whoever she or he might be, was wide awake; the pack wriggled violently against the woman's chest. Staring now, trying to figure out what sort of tiny one could emit that much force and energy, I saw a tail a emerge from the bottom of the pack, and my breath stopped. "Oh my God," I thought, "She forgot the baby!" Okay, so it wasn't my brightest morning, but never having seen such a thing before, I couldn't quite process a pup in a Baby Bjorn.

The woman crossed over to the opposite side of North Street and headed into one of our newer restaurants, puppy in pack, and my disbelief grew. We don't live in Paris, where furry creatures sit at tables. We live in New England, where dogs are firmly relegated to back yards, and specific parks, and beaches only for certain hours. We have rules here in the cold north, and puppies in sushi restaurants are definitely a rule violation. I rushed over to her side of the street to stalk her. I had to know. Why a puppy? Why sushi?

I entered the restaurant, halted at the host station, and saw that the woman and her fur ball had been seated at a corner table. The pup's head was out of the pack, smelling everything he could get his sniffer on, and the woman appeared to be calmly mumbling to the dog, perhaps reading the menu to him ... who knows what she was doing ... I still thought she might be a bit crazy. The manager came over and asked calmly, as if nothing unusual was happening at all, "Table for one?"

I stared at him for a moment.

"No, not interested," I replied, sweeping my arm toward the woman. "I'm stalking her."

The manager laughed, as if I were the odd one, and invited me to go on over to her, saying I would enjoy this.

I crossed through the tables, put my hand out, introduced myself to the woman and told her, without chagrin, that I had to know what she was doing with what looked like a cocker spaniel in a front pack, having an early lunch. She laughed, and gestured for me to sit and told me her name. It didn't register. She had become irrelevant. I was focused on the pup and the story that had gotten him into that cotton sling.

The doggy, all of perhaps ten pounds, leaned toward me, squirmed with his whole body, licked my hands, yelped for more surface area to lick while his owner began to explain. Turns out she trains dogs to visit stroke patients. In certain hospitals, we can now bring dogs into stroke wards, who made that up?? When this pup is fully trained, she will bring him to our local hospital, place him on the side of a patient's bed or even on his or her chest, and watch the magic happen.

"Really?"

I had begun to consider stealing the spaniel, his affection was so enthusiastic, so incredibly delicious.

"Uh huh!"

A stroke patient, even a depressed one, will often work hard to move to pet a puppy. They can't help themselves and in so doing they begin a faster journey toward recovery than if they are simply given physical therapy instructions.

"Many people, even when they are really frustrated, they'll move to try to feel the puppy under their hands. Especially if we put the dog on their chests, right on top of their hearts," she continued. "I bring the pups to restaurants to get them used to sudden noise and a mix of people so they are ready for hospital rooms."

A puppy on their hearts. I looked at the dog, clearly delighted in his position in the world. He was thrilled to be out meeting new people, smelling the air for all it had to offer, happy to have a job to do that was fully resonant with his purpose in life: to love a whole lot of folk as much as he could.

After staying for a few moments, I headed back out.

I found a table at the coffee shop, sat down to write about resilience and only one sentence emerged.

"I want a puppy against my heart."

I want to feel that kind of aliveness, that unconditionally positive, hand-licking brand of love, right in front of me. I want to bring that kind of kindness to my own heart and to this world. I want to walk into a shop, and have the world be lit up by the pure force of gladness embodied by spaniel pups because I am that dog and I want the world to know what he already knew ... it is okay always to be in joy. It is okay always to be in wonder with the smells of the world, the new faces around you, and bring to bodies and souls that have suffered a heart undefended and free, wrigglingly happy and constantly, relentlessly warm.

An open heart is required.

So much of the time ours are caged.

Here is the question we could bring to our days: "If I had the heart of a spaniel, how might I greet this moment?"

Or how about this one: "If I wagged my way through this doorway, what might happen next?"

Imagine then the ease that might come to the person right in front of us, and the soothing of our own wounds. Imagine how the day might have a bit more light to it, and the moment in front of us might seem slightly more interesting as if its smells and sounds and textures were — well — fascinating. We just might find ourselves transported ... out of the labyrinthine tunnels of our usually neurotic minds ... and into states of temporary enthrallment where even restaurants are amazing and hospital wards not so dreary and the crossing of ordinary streets an adventure.

I am not suggesting a naïve pretense here or a Hollywood-like suspension of reality. Rather an invitation to consider the following: few creatures are more gifted at celebrating the very moment of living in front of us than a puppy. In its undefended state it finds the day wondrous.

"This," to quote my dear friend, Cynthia, "might not be such a bad thing."

"I'm not telling you to make the world better ... I'm just telling you to live in it."

~Joan Didion

This Meeting,
One Chance

Sen no Rikyū, tea master of the 16th century, is known for his poetic and philosophic understanding of the import of the Japanese tea ceremony, and he can be best understood through the lens of a small fierce command central to his philosophy: *This meeting, one chance.* This life, one opportunity. There is no other reality. And even when that life is rampant with pain, terrorist attacks, and police brutality, or, like yesterday, over the border in my neighboring town, a tragic death of a young girl in a car driven by a drunken teen, this reality remains fixed. In this form, we have one shot. Even those of us who believe in life after death or the karmic wheel or the transfer of energy from one form to another can agree on this: as we exist, we have only this meeting.

Happiness requires both pleasure and meaning...that which brings a smile to our faces and that which brings a deep sense of purpose to our lives. We must have both, in a balance that is unique and authentic for each of us.

What powers pleasure, however, and the expression of meaning is a commitment to dive in, to seize the moment, as Didion writes, and to live in life. Not around it. Not beside it. Not running away from it or relentlessly controlling it, but to live full-on in life. Anne Lamott writes about finding the "wedding in the day", and Annie Dillard reminds us to "Spend it all. Shoot it, play it, lose it, every time." These writers seem to be onto the same wisdom Rikyū laid out for us oh so long ago: there is no time but now. Our choice is to dive in or hold back. Take the shot or sit in the far dark corner allowing others to play the game.

We can spend hours thinking about what brings pleasure to our days or meaning. We can make lists, call friends, talk to our therapist, and journal for endless evenings, on lined and unlined pages, making plans to make a plan to actually begin to act on that which makes us happy, or we can get up off the couch. Happiness requires action. It demands of us thought, this is true, and consciousness, but most of all the clear, direct movement of doing the thing.

When John died, I began to dance at 6am in my den to MTV and VHI. Dancing made me happy. The early hour spared me from commentary by my lovely and opinionated teens. It shifted my naturally anxious, depressive mindset and shifted me into a positive territory. It freed me from rumination and reminded me that I was young enough to still move and therefore I could move toward more than the rock star music of the day, I could move into life and see and taste and touch and feel. It helped me understand that at our best we are dancing with life...allowing it to lead and then choosing to lead. We can choose the music and the tempo and see how life responds. Life and me. Me and life. Together.

I danced for 13 months. That's how long it took to begin to know that I had come into a new world that began to feel normal and that John's death was no longer something I fought or despaired about but walked with each day, just as I walk with my own heart and my own lungs. He, the fullness of him, is within me now and close. My choice to practice each day something that brought me great pleasure enabled me to remember that even on days of blackness I have a choice. I could wallow or rise.

The grave is a fine and private place, affirms Didion. Soon enough we will know this for ourselves. But not today. Not in this moment. This moment, this meeting, we have the opportunity to lean into life, even if only for ten minutes or four or one minute a day, in such a way that we are alive, really and truly living.

"Concerning all acts of initiative (and creation), there is one elementary truth..: that the moment one definitely commits oneself, then Providence moves too ... Whatever you can do, or dream you can do, begin it. Boldness has genius, power, and magic in it. Begin it now."

~ William Hutchison Murray

The World Will Rise to Meet You

There is a faith possible in the universe, one not necessarily connected to divinity or even a sense of the sacred, but a faith spoken of and known by many. It's an understanding that as we move toward a life that nourishes us, the world will rise to meet us. It will send envoys of sorts, carriers of messages that essentially say, "You are on the right path. Keep going. The universe is with you." As we choose to take action that is positive, nourishing, and in alignment with our true and healthy selves, it can sometimes appear as if the world is right there with us on the journey, calling us forward into who we might become. This is such a lovely faith to believe in ... a beautiful cup to drink from and a hopeful one as well ... and as we drink here we necessarily drink also from the cup of optimism and the vessel of connection.

Faith of this sort implies that there is some kind of energy in the world that is supporting us; that we aren't alone even though we might sometimes feel lonely.

I have known this faith. Its evidence has been palpable during the easiest passages in my life, and, I have learned to seek it as well during the darkest times. If we keep our eyes soft and our hearts open, we too may see the adjustments the universe makes on our behalf.

A student of mine, after a week of work together, committed to doing a daily yoga practice to begin her journey of healing. On the last day of our work together, she changed her mind as she realized there was neither time nor space in her home for even ten minutes of yoga per day. She believed she would fail and so chose instead to focus on making one healthy meal a day. That would be her next best step into her journey of greater wellbeing. She hadn't spoken to her husband that week about her thoughts and so I encouraged her to connect with him on the way home to bring him into agreement about her desire for healthy dinners each night. She called him. He agreed. On the way home that Friday night she bought healthy food at Whole Foods. They made a great meal together and as the evening began to cool she headed inside to their junk room to find a sweater.

She walked up the stairs, turned the corner, went to open the door of the junk room and saw a sign on the door, "Martha's Room." The hair on the back of her neck went up. She opened the door, assuming she would see the piles of clothes, papers, boots, winter gear that had crowded that room for months. Instead she saw this: clear floors, a yoga mat, a candle and a CD player. In shock she ran back downstairs, said to her husband, "What?" "How did you know I really wanted to do a yoga practice but I couldn't imagine clearing a space for it?"

He answered: "When you left on Sunday night for your retreat it occurred to me that you would need a quiet space to come home to. That night the kids and I began emptying the room."

She hadn't told him that yoga would become her first-choice pathway into healing...and yet somehow he had known even before she did. The world rose to meet her.

Deepak Chopra calls this synchrodestiny and Wayne Dyer encouraged us to look for the signs each day, those as small as butterflies and as large as spouses who reshape our homes for us. The Dalai Lama offers, "I am open to the guidance of synchronicity and do not let expectations hinder my path." He does not, in other words, allow his strategic mind or his expectations to limit his understanding of life's potential, nor does he refuse to see the mysterious coincidences that are simply incredible and somewhat unbelievable, unless we hold open the possibility that life finds a way to align with us.

Perhaps this is divine intervention. Perhaps this is a complicated sort of quantum physics of energy alignment. Perhaps we have a latent ability within us to recognize patterns or connections which becomes sharper and more developed as we begin to actively seek out those patterns. Or perhaps some things are impossible to fully comprehend. What I do know is that often the happier among us share an openness to what is possible; a willingness to consider, if only now and then, that at any moment wondrous, ineffable surprises can occur.

In my first experience of great despair, when my world fell apart in my 20s, a friend suggested I buy a journal and write about my experiences in order to gain perspective. I suspect, too, that she had had enough of my ruminations with her over tea. One sunny day that spring I drove to the Unicorn Bookstore in Arlington, Massachusetts, a suburb of Boston. I parked my car, went inside and spent nearly 90 minutes shopping. Who knew there were hundreds of journaling books? Lined, unlined, bound, wire bound, leather covered, cloth, tiny, huge; the choices overwhelmed me. The printing of the Gutenberg Bible took less time than I took to pick a book. After a thousand minutes I chose: a green cloth-covered book, with an embossed word on the cover, "Woodnotes," and inside a stanza from Emerson's poem of the same name. I love trees. They make me happy. It felt like exactly the right choice.

I paid for the journal, headed to my car, and stopped. From a distance of ten yards I could see a branch on my Honda's hood. A branch, not a twig. It ran the width of my hood and had numerous little branches running off it. At its thickest it measured the size of my thigh...not a huge thigh, but a thigh not a forearm. I stared at the thing. I thought, "Oh there must have been a storm." But no evidence of a storm existed. The day had remained dry and sunny. I thought, "I must have parked under a tree." A delusional thought. No tree stood anywhere near my car. Then this idea: "Maybe the tree guys had come by and dropped a branch on my car." That's how nutty my thinking became because tree guys tend to demolish their trimmings with those massive steel chewing devices they trot around with, not leave branches on parked cars.

I found no way to make sense of this moment. It was as if I had been transported without my knowledge into another universe ... one that appeared exactly the same except for that strange wood bit on my car.

I walked back into the shop. My face must have looked stricken because the shopkeeper came right over to ask what had happened. I told her about the branch. Pulled the journal back out of the bag she had placed it in. Lifted the cover to show her that one word, "Woodnotes," and said, "I don't understand."

She laughed. "Oh this stuff happens all the time!"

"Trees out of nowhere happen all the time?"

"Evidence," she replied, clearly delighted. "Evidence that you are on the right path."

The moment one commits oneself, in little ways and large, Providence moves too.

"Our lives are like movies: we have to edit them to create a coherent story. But sometimes we need to go back to the unused footage to find material for a better version. A better version of ourselves."

~ *Margarita Tarragona*

A New Story...

Years ago, I sat with eight fourth graders who were having a very hard time editing an essay draft. Once they had squeezed a sentence out, they absolutely couldn't imagine changing it or improving it. It was hard enough figuring out those first ten words. Late in the day on a winter afternoon, we squished into a circle and I told them how the imagination sometimes needs time to kick in. Our minds can surprise us with what suddenly appears in a story, but we have to give it a chance to warm up, like the new energy-saving lights — they begin dim and then glow brighter and brighter. Editing is the chance for the bright glow to appear, for the work to get better as we give it time and attention. I asked them, diligent nine-year-olds with scrubby pencils and bitten erasers in hand, to hunker down on the carpet, take out their notebooks, and see what new might emerge. The group, silent and serious, settled in, and stared at their sentences willing something novel to show itself.

One girl, Emma, a lover of writing, slammed her belly to the floor and put her nose right above her notebook. Had she glared any harder at her work, it would have melted. Minutes passed. She twirled her hair and sighed loudly. She tapped her pencil on the edge of the page. Other children wrote, crossed out words, ripped out pages. She stared. Other children crafted paragraphs, dialogue, one hummed as his pencil skidded along. She remained fixed, frozen. Time passed; a lot of time. I worried for her. Suddenly, Emma sat up. She pulled her notebook to her knees. I watched her circle her opening sentence, draw an arrow down to the bottom of the page, and dash something off. She looked up at me then, her forehead crunched, her eyebrows tight and wrinkled. I nodded and held out my hand; she gave me her notebook. Her original first sentence read: "I want to live in California where it is warm all the time." The bottom of the page showed this: "I love my life because everyday the sun warms everything and it doesn't matter where you are or if other kids like you."

Every day the sun warms everything; there is a way to love your life.

Each morning the sun does its thing, offering us its fealty. Our job is to become aware of that rising, holding it as a grace or at least a gift — the gift of assurance that time continues and warmth exists and our days, even those of harshness and emptiness, can begin anew.

Happiness after loss is not about everything that we want suddenly appearing or about the past being rewritten as if our sisters were never raped, or our work never fell apart, or our houses did not ever burn. It's about our re-storying the present moment through a new lens, one in which we recognize the bounty that is already present and the possibility of a new normal that includes both our torment and the gifts in front of us.

There is a way to love your life, and this is most true as we find a way to love the life right in front of us ... the constant sun, the rhapsody of color, the boundlessness of sound. We may despise what has happened, be terrified of the future or beset with despair and yet, still, the world exists for us to experience anew, as if it were here to be played with, as if through its own eternal resurrection from night to day to night, and then day, it would like us to understand that the very nature of living is one of integration, dis-integration, surprising growth, and integration again. This is the way of the mortal life; it is what is. We can choose to become resonant with this organic flow of living by seeing, truly seeing its plenty. From that place we find a new story, written directly from the shattered pieces of the old.

Here is Jacques Lusseyran, author of *And There Was Light*. Blinded in a schoolroom accident at the age of eight, he went from 'normal' to an unusual life and in that altered story came to delight in his capacity to be with the world anew, in this instance through the gift of sound:

"Sight is a miraculous instrument ... but we receive nothing in the world without paying for it, and in return for all the benefits that sight brings we are forced to give up others whose existence we don't even expect. These were the gifts [of sound] I received in such abundance. I needed to hear and hear again. I multiplied sounds to my heart's content. I rang bells. I touched walls with my fingers, explored the resonance of doors, furniture and trunks of trees ... I threw pebbles far off on the beach just to hear them whistle through the air and then fall ... with sound I never came to an end, for this was another kind of infinity."

This is what is possible ... another kind of infinity. A new way constructed from the ashes of the old. "I built my new life from love," affirms Madonna Badger, even as the wounds from that Christmas Eve fire laced her heart.

In my brother's home, his children are living full lives ... graduate school, college, friends, and work. They wear the rings he crafted for them, his presence kept near. We grieve deeply still, yet there is no going back. We each compose the next chapter of our living. Often, when I visit I choose to stand on his stoop and remember the sight of those high school and middle school friends crossing the road the morning John died. Their love held us all that day and the resonance of their generosity is as palpable still as is the spirit of my brother. Looking back now I can see that their kindness became the first traceline of healing on my heart, a golden joining. From that bare shimmer of amity, and my choice to see it, hold on to it, and live as if it mattered, I have been able craft a life that included my deepest sorrow yet and also a burgeoning joy.

A Final Note

Our world is as it has always been.

These examples, my losses and strains, the stories of my clients, students, teachers, and the poets, present a small sampling of what has been true through time and will always be. We each suffer. No one is spared.

What happened once upon a time in darkness happens again and again.

And what happened once in joy or serenity or awe happens again and again. None of us is spared this truth as well.

We cannot possibly predict the trauma yet to come to us nor the beneficence.

If we keep our minds open, our eyes soft, our hearts lined with the wisdom of choices that heal and offer uplift, we may find our way into that place where we are shattered and lined with gold, scarred and yet whole.

There will be dying, confirms poet Derek Mahon...and the sun rises in spite of everything.

Notes to Self

"Give sorrow words. The grief that does not speak whispers the o'er-fraught heart and bids it break."

~Shakespeare

Notes to Self

"But I also say this: that light is an invitation to happiness, and that happiness, when it's done right, is a kind of holiness, palpable and redemptive."

~*Mary Oliver*

Suggested Resources

"A Broken Body is Not a Broken Person," TED Talk, Janine Shepard, Aug. 2012

And There Was Light, Jacques Lusseyran, New World Library, March 2014

An Exact Replica of a Figment of My Imagination, Elizabeth McCracken, Back Bay Books, Feb. 2010

Bird by Bird, Anne Lamott, Anchor, Sept. 1995

Happier, Tal Ben-Shahar, McGraw Hill Education, May 2007

Man's Search for Meaning, Viktor Frankl, Beacon Press, June 2006

Positive Identities: Narrative Practices and Positive Psychology, Margarita Tarragona, CreateSpace Independent Publishing Platform, March 2013

Radically Receptive Meditation, Megan McDonough, Wholebeing Institute, 2015

The Writing Life, Annie Dillard, Harper Perennial, Nov. 2013

A Short Course in Happiness, Lynda Wallace, Three Sixty Five, Feb. 2013

The Anatomy of Hope, Jerome Groopman, Random House Trade Paperbacks, Jan. 2005

The Blessing of a Broken Heart, Sherri Mandell, Toby Press, Jan. 2009

The Gifts of Imperfection, Brene Brown, Hazeldon, Aug. 2010

The Journal Keeper, Phyllis Theroux, Grove Press, March 2011

The Year of Magical Thinking, Joan Didion, Vintage, Feb. 2007

When Things Fall Apart, Pema Chodron, Shambala, Sept. 2000

When You Are Falling, Dive, Mark Matousek, CreateSpace Independent Publishing Platform, June 2008

Acknowledgments

A few years ago Lynda Wallace, a colleague of mine, wrote a book, *A Short Course in Happiness*, which has helped many recreate their lives. I want to thank her first for her generous permission to use her title as a foundation and take it elsewhere, and for her wise appreciation of brevity as a keystone to this work. We all rest on the shoulders of those before us ... thank you for allowing me to rest on yours.

Janet Reich Elsbach has been the godmother of this project, in her keen care for sentences and her willingness to allow me into her heart ever more deeply as grief came and settled in her kitchen. To be continued, darling ...

Carrie Owens, thank you for all those mornings at the café, as we wrote in silence together. Your devotion to your own work became the field in which this one could finally be born. Thank you...the first next cup is on me!

To Phyllis Theroux, writing teacher, mentor, and friend, who told me twice to throw away work that was broken and asked me the question that triggered the evolution of this writing: "Instead of telling us what happened when your brother died, can you show us what it taught you?" I am devoted to the fellowship we have created.

To Tal Ben-Shahar, I owe you more than can be written here. Thank you for bringing so much wisdom to our time, for having the courage to show us your vision and write it down, and for inviting me along on the journey.

To Megan McDonough, thank you for stepping into your leadership so that so many of us might step into ours more fully. Here's to a work and life of wholeness and health and laughter!!

To Jennifer Browdy, Jana Laiz, and the Green Fire team, I'm so happy we did this one together. It's been such a delight and a relief to work with smart, passionate, lively, and full-hearted women!

To those who join me in this work, my students, teaching assistants, colleagues, and clients, you cannot know how your desire to grow inspires the same in me and turns the swamp of life into a place of burgeoning beauty. I am in your debt. May we serve our work forward together for decades and decades to come...like forever.

To my huge, extended, complicated, deeply bonded family, the seeds of my resilience began with you all and will continue to grow because of the choices we have made to hang in there together. Bless you and us for that and for both the shit and shine that no one could possibly make up.

To my friends, I could not do this without you; it's as simple as that. I owe you my sanity and a huge piece of my joy...as well as a thousand meals. One day I'll feed you more than words, but I wouldn't hold my breath for that in this lifetime. Until that time, know that I am so happy to serve the good you help me find right back to you in every other way. Love, love, love.

To H.M.K, the only proper response to a gift such as you is thank you. To see the world through your eyes is to see goodness, to be near your warm embrace is to feel hope and to be invited into to your heart is heaven, the real kind, where we get to be imperfect and fumble about and be held as worthy anyway. I am the luckiest woman alive.

R. and J., I'm not sure why I seek to protect your identity a bit here when I throw you under the bus regularly when I teach, but there it is; you do you,

I'll do me. Thank you for showing up as you have all these years, exactly as you are, and for teaching me that love truly is in the dailiness of helping each other find our own ways through this life thing without having to go it alone. My heart is as large as the universe because of you. Your courageous love, R., is a sanctuary so many of us climb into each day, and your constant warmth, J., heals many more than you know. The idea for this work happened after I lost your uncle, but the heart of this book is to provide a roadmap for you for that time when I can no longer smother you with care. 'Til then, sad to say my darlings, my quirky, tenacious, imperfect mothering will continue. Make good choices, my loves, and floss.

Dr. Maria Sirois is a clinical psychologist, international consultant and inspirational speaker who works in the intersections of psychology and wellbeing. She is a master teacher and facilitator, devoted to the science of happiness and the art of crafting a life and a work that embodies health, passion and success. As a positive psychologist and consultant, she focuses on the resilience of the human spirit, particularly when under chronic stress and/or the shock of things falling apart. Her first book, *Every Day Counts: Lessons in Love, Faith and Resilience From Children Facing Illness* is used as a teaching tool at wellness centers, hospitals and hospices and offers wisdom from those who are dying. Her home is in the Berkshire Mountains.

For more information about Maria's work, visit
WWW.MARIASIROIS.COM

Made in the USA
Middletown, DE
23 May 2016

32106460R00114